HIGHLAND AIR

HIGHLAND AIR
A Farmer's Diary

BEN COUTTS

ABERDEEN UNIVERSITY PRESS
Member of Maxwell Macmillan Pergamon Publishing

First published 1990
Aberdeen University Press

© Ben Coutts 1990

British Library Cataloguing in Publication Data

Coutts, Ben *1916–*
　　Highland air.
　　1. Scotland, history
　　I. Title
　　630.9411

　　ISBN 0 08 037976 1

Printed in Great Britain at BPCC-AUP Aberdeen Ltd. Member of BPCC Ltd.

FOREWORD

I am glad Aberdeen University Press are publishing a selection of Ben's broadcasts over the years. Ben Coutts is, and has been, one of the most inseeing of commentators on the agricultural scene for 40 years. His great virtue is that he is not only a penetrating and intelligent observer of Scottish rural life and agriculture, but he makes his living off the land and is himself a leader in many fields. It is the combination of the practical with the ability to communicate which is so valuable. I have enjoyed his friendship for many years, and his appetite for life is a joy to behold. Few people have such a width of experience, from reluctant scholar to pony boy, a wartime career which he was extremely lucky to survive, his wide experience in farming, broadcasting, administration, local and national politics. These make him as unique an observer as he is a person. The broadcasts are valuable and, even better, enjoyable.

Lord Mackie of Benshie, CBE, DSO, DFC, LLD,
Liberal Democrat Spokesman on Agriculture in the House of Lords

Even Solomon in all his glory was not arrayed like
one of these: drawn by Caroline Brett.

ACKNOWLEDGEMENTS

In his introduction to *Bothy to Big Ben* Max Hastings was kind enough to say that I could have been a professional broadcaster instead of being 'well known on Highland air waves'. I doubt his prediction but if the latter is true perhaps some people will enjoy reading some of my fortnightly ramblings that they missed on Highland Air.

Pat Chalmers, Controller BBC Scotland, not only gave me permission to have some of Ben Coutts' Diaries published but wished me well. Thanks, Pat.

To many producers over the past 40 years but especially the most recent batch - Alan Wright, Charlie Allan, Ken Rundle, Freida Morrison and Jan Gavin - I know you should come first, Ladies, but I've done it in the sequence that you produced me.

To my favourite adopted niece, Brett, and my sister Maisie who have done such lovely sketches depicting the countryside and seasons - as one who can't draw anything at all I can't thank you enough.

My old friend Me Lord George Mackie, for his more than kind words of introduction and finally to Colin MacLean who once more has had enough faith in my writing to think that the book was worth publishing, my thanks.

BC

These broadcast talks, given over several years in the late 1980s, reflect more than half a century on the land. As is apparent from some of the references to people and events, the talks are not presented here in the chronological sequence in which they were broadcast. Apart from 'Far From the Crowd' they are grouped under calendar months in which they were given.

January

How things have changed at the Festive Season! I don't have to worry now about early rising over Christmas and New Year. I always took on feeding the beasts during that period, preferring to take my days' holiday at other times of the year.

Now I am worshipping again of a Sunday at the wee 'Bunty pulls the strings' type church that I joined in 1944 when I was bailed out of the forces because of my wounds. 'Unfit for further service' - sounds rather like a vet's report on an old horse. I was lucky enough to land a plum farm manager's job in lovely Strathearn. I employed five married men on that farm and there were two single Irish men in the bothy for harvest and tattie dressing time. Needless to say, there is only one man on that farm today. In those days we worked on Christmas Day and the men all went first footing each other and their neighbours at New Year - and pretty useless they were for a day or two afterwards. One never saw a Christmas tree in a cottage window and as for a Christmas Eve service, one would be laughed to scorn if one suggested it. Now the wee Kirk is well-nigh full on Christmas Eve and laymen and women conduct the service. Every cottage and house has its Christmas tree, children get wildly expensive presents, (thanks to our higher standard of living) and first footing, thanks to the Breathalyser, is a shadow of its former self. Even the beasts on many farms are on a self-feed system and don't need early morning attention. Are we better off than of yore? I'm told by many first class farmers that the first thing they do if they are in financial difficulties is make a man redundant. The stamp contributions, the six weeks holiday etc make contract labour very attractive.

I've had two outstanding meals, apart from Christmas dinner, during the past fortnight. The first was a present of steak from a butcher friend. He had bought this cattle beast that had been turned down as overfat. He rightly guessed that it would have a large proportion of red meat. So it proved as I saw it hanging up and it had the best round of Pope's Eye I've ever seen and it melted in my mouth. The other was a gigot that I ate on the Borders from a cross Suffolk that had been turned down as over fat. Again, it tasted delicious. I'm heartily fed up being told that if I eat cholesterol I'll shorten my life. It's time this crazy grading system was abolished or sorted out once and for all and that should be one of every NFU Council member's New Year resolutions. Otherwise our meat eating public will be frightened away by chewing tough and tasteless meat and only the dentists will benefit as the whole country will need new snappers.

1

January

I am looking out of my north facing window at the foothills of the Grampians, deep in snow, and the wintry sun shining on them reminding me of the icing on the Christmas cake with the electric light reflected on its surface.

My heart goes out to the hill boys battling their way through drifts to feed their beasts. I had my share when from 1951-59 I farmed Gaskbeg up in Badenoch. One day I'll particularly remember. I was tenant of the farm and having come out of the army with a £70 gratuity, which was spent on furniture for my first manager's home in 1944, I was indebted to the late Duncan Stewart of Millhills, Messrs MacDonald Fraser and the bank for allowing me to become tenant of the farm. I always remember the late Lovat Fraser's remark 'You look honest Ben and Duncan gives you a good reference but you only get money from us if you buy and sell everything through our mart *and* you keep a flock of sheep and a herd of cows'. Sound advice that many farmers in financial trouble would have been wise to follow these past few years.

I had been tenant for only three years when a knock came to the door and this was one of my neighbouring tenants to say that our landlord was in temporary financial trouble and he, the tenant, had bought the farming end of the Estate and he didn't want my farm or the two other tenanted farms beside me, and so cheap had he bought the lot that I could have the three for £5,000 which although money values were different in the 1950s was still cheap. Just imagine my excitement - from the Bothy in the 'thirties to being Laird of Lagganbridge in the 'fifties. Heady stuff indeed. The first thing I decided was to borrow the money from one source only so I phoned up my bank manager in Crieff, told him the story and fixed an appointment.

It was one of those winters that Badenoch dwellers know so well. The water was constantly frozen. One would open the back door of a morning and a snow drift would cascade inside. The byre was the only warm place and how I loved to go out last thing at night with a storm lantern and look at the cows chained by the neck, munching their beautifully smelling meadow hay. The dam of Highland Princess champion at the Scottish and National Smithfield was one of them that fateful year. The hinds too came down to within a few hundred yards of the steading to pick up any strands of hay that the out-wintered cattle had left, but on the morning in question although there were a few hundred within shot I had no time to do anything about it as I was rushing. It was the year of the doubles. In those spacious days I employed

2

two men, and a boy as well in the summer. The two men were sick, one with double pneumonia and the other with a double hernia, hence the year of the doubles, and hence my early start to feeding. But I had everything done by the time it was light, which of course was after eight, and I went to Newtonmore as the hill road to Dalwhinnie was blocked and it was still snowing. The van was fairly ancient but luckily was highly sprung and of course in those days had chains on the rear tyres. As I headed up the dreaded Drumochter Pass, which even today has problems, I knew I was in for trouble and so it proved. Those super railwaymen who in the old days lived at the quaintly named Balsporran dug me out, and when I told them my mission they came with me over the top of the summit saying they'd get back with the railway snowplough. After a hair raising journey I reached Crieff hours late; having got up at 3 a.m. I was a bit wabbit but still in high spirits with the thought of being Laird. The bank manager was just leaving but took me inside and with a steely look in his eye said "I phoned up headquarters and they looked up the map and as your farm house is 1,000 ft above sea level they aren't interested and anyway your overdraft is ridiculously high at £170".

January

I could have sworn that bank manager's eye was a glass one. Looking back after all those years, it may have been a shattering blow to my conceit as I thought the bank and their manager were being uncaring and hadn't done their homework about the Badenoch area. But comparing it with the lush farms of the eastern seaboard, perhaps they were right. Anyway I'm a great fatalist, and I'm a happy man.

This is the month of dinners, Burns Suppers, Annual General Meetings, you name it - but an awful lot of hot air will be expended. Over the past forty years I suppose I've contributed my share towards, shall we say, 'warming the atmosphere' (it sounds better than hot air).

I've been trying to give up most of my public speaking, for many reasons. Many people don't realise just how much preparation a speech takes nor how much nervous energy it take out of one. After forty years the butterflies in my tummy get larger rather then less. And these broadcast diary extracts - which I enjoy doing so much - take a full day between thought of subject matter, writing it, going to a studio and back. Plus the nervous tension which I have all day prior to the broadcast. Sounds stupid, but it's true.

Then over the years unthinking secretaries send almost peremptory letters, often just stating 'my committee have decided that they wish you to be principal speaker at our etc etc.' All too often without even enclosing a stamped addressed envelope and sometimes even requesting a potted biography of myself (if they don't know about me I can't think why they would want me to speak). When I think of the thousands of miles I've travelled and have seldom even been offered expenses! A gentle reminder to any secretaries of any bodies who are looking for speakers - a wee bit of thought will improve the type of speaker you get.

There was no thought of expenses in my mind but only sadness when I had to do two appreciations at two funerals recently, the first Will Hogg of Clackmae and the second Robin Fisher originally from Balimore, Balquidder but who lived in Sussex all his working life. Robin it was who got me my first farm manager's job just before the outbreak of war so I owed him a debt it would be hard to repay.

4

January

I went to Sussex by train. Very warm and comfortable it was and I was able to study the farming on the way down. Two things struck me, firstly the fantastic acreage of winter crops that have been sown, I suppose thanks to the good autumn weather, and I only hope for the growers' sake there's another drought in Europe next summer. And secondly, the number of sheep that are now on arable farms where they haven't been seen for half a century. It bodes ill for the hill and upland men (who can produce only mutton and wool) unless something is put in motion *now* to safeguard them.

Neither Will nor Robin were kirk greedy but they both loved nature and were thankful for their lot - and I think most farmers would agree with the sentiments of the Cowboy's Prayer:

> I ain't much good at prayin', and you may not know me, Lord
> I ain't much seen in churches where they preach Thy Holy Word,
> But you may have seen me out here on the lonely plains,
> A-lookin' after cattle, feelin' thankful when it rains.

January

Admirin' Thy great handiwork, the miracle of grass,
Aware of Thy kind spirit in the way it comes to pass
That hired men on horseback and the livestock that we tend
Can look up at the stars at night and know we've got a Friend.

January is not only the month for Burns' Suppers but also for NFU and agricultural show AGMs and dinners. I was saddened indeed to hear that one NFU branch with which I had been connected had lost nine members this year - not by death, or retirement from farming, but because they thought that enough wasn't being done for them by the Union! One member who farms extremely well - and with two farms - had the lame excuse that he couldn't afford the sub! Having served my stint on NFU Committees and Council I realise that like all institutions and bodies it has its faults. But surely now, as never before, the farming industry should be speaking with one voice as we are assailed from all sides by all sorts of Weirdies who would be the first to shout if they run short of food but seem to think that they know how to manage the country's greatest asset, the land, better than those of us who have spent a lifetime doing just that.

Our local show held its AGM seething openly, because a county show had altered its midweek date onto our Saturday, which we have stuck to for years - yes even when three years running we hit the wettest Saturdays on record. But we've kept our heads above water, literally and financially, and mean to take on the big guns with our bows and arrows. Why bows and arrows? Because we're all Indians. Our show had a wonderful way of cutting one down to size. I was Chairman one year, Chief scaffie the next, picking up those horrible sticky sweetie papers, and on the gates the next at 6.30 a.m., arguing with a small minority of the entrants who think one small pony needs half a dozen attendants.

The old saying goes that 'the grass is always greener over the fence' and until this year I have always thought it so as I'd dig myself out or slither to the railway station for the January Smithfield Club 'greetin' meetin' only to find the South of England basked in sunshine or at worst every farmer still ploughing. But not so this year when I left a fairly mild climate to go to London which was enjoying about 6-8 degrees of frost.

January

The poor old southerners, you'd think the end of the world had come when they get a cold week. I spent a night in Oxfordshire visiting an 83-year-old widow of a former boss and the huge house she lives in was like a morgue (and I was glad of my Inverness cape to cover my feet in bed) and all the water troughs had been left on and her beloved Shetland ponies were without water. I wonder what they'd do if they experienced some of the storms that we get.

This thought prompted me to think of the imbalance that is going on and always seems to go on in farming between big farmers in the lush arable acres of the east, now known as the 'fat cats', and the wee family hill farmer for whom I have so much time. Once again the latter have suffered as the Capital Grants Scheme, which has done so much for the hills, has been slashed from 50% to 30% in many cases whereas the white crop of which we seem to grow too much, thanks to modern varieties and techniques, is to be cut back a mere 3.5%. Which meant that some of the big boys won't enjoy two Porches but have to do with one plus a B M W.

I think the family farm will be the salvation of farming in the U K. Why? Because they have their feet on the ground and dung on their boots and they are the people who, in this district at any rate, still have a rotation and don't create barley deserts. They look after their dykes, ditches, drains and fences and they are the answer to the conservationists who are becoming more and more strident in their lobbying.

Old Ben has another bee in his bonnet you may say. Well tell me why drystane dykes and shelter belts now qualify for a 70% grant whereas scrub and boulder clearance for re-seeding are out the window grant-wise. Quite simply because of the conservation lobby. We shrug those lobbies off at our peril. They are going to gather more and more forces as our surpluses get bigger.

What about some of the Forestry projects that have been allowed? There is now a 50,000 acre block from Amulree to Aberfeldy, one of the biggest in Europe, and blotting out one of the loveliest car runs in Scotland. But it's the old story. All too often the farmer who knows most about the problems is too busy farming and can't get off to speak his mind or perhaps isn't good at public speaking.

One of the tasks I have performed for the Royal Smithfield Club is to represent them on the Nuffield Scholarship Committee. Farming listeners will know that Nuffield Scholarships are eagerly sought after by young and not so young farmers. I got mine to New Zealand, Australia and South Africa for two months at the age of 49! With a changing agriculture and a Third World crying out for better agricultural facilities I suggested to the Nuffield Scholarship Committee that perhaps they ought to review their policy and instead of sending students to the States, Canada, Europe they should let some come home to show us how to grow more. They should still send at least some to Africa to show them how to grow more. This may seem mean of me when I gained so much from the trip but I would gladly have gone to drought stricken countries had I been asked (and as I was resident in Argyll in 1964 I was pretty knowledgeable about rain!). Sadly I had to report to Smithfield Council my idea was turned down flat.

One way or another, I've been connected with farming now for well over half a century. Since I 'hung up my boots' I've really missed my house cow. There is something therapeutic about nestling one's head up to a cow's warm belly on a cold winter's morning and listening to the hiss of milk on the froth and also to the cow munching her feed, That's when I planned the day's work. The byre was always so welcoming with its pigs grunting and that lovely warmth, and the animal smells that greeted one. I could never see why economists always maintain that house cows don't pay.

I've reared two families on decent tasty milk, none of this pasteurised homogenised nonsense, and my six children (four now with their own children) moaned like mad if they had to drink the licensed water now too often sold as milk when the coo went dry. We made enough butter to keep us most of the year. Yes, that lovely yellow stuff that one can make only from grass that isn't clobbered with nitrogen. In fact I often grazed the coo down the long meadow - the farm road.

The pigs, five in all, a pair, then another pair, then a single. They were fed on skim milk and oats. Two conveniently died so far as my accountant was concerned but landed in my deep freeze and tasted completely different from the bacon and ham one gets full of barley and fish meal, as was borne out by the fact that I regularly topped the Perth Market with the ones I sold. Wandering through one's beasts and seeing how one's crops are faring are a constant joy. For me stock has always come before crop.

We now have hens, dogs and Highland ponies which I need to get up in the morning to feed and to exercise. A good thing, as all too many retired farmers of my acquaintance have gone into the local town and have suddenly ceased to work physically. Their names appear in the Death column in all too short a time.

One thing I don't miss in retirement are the ever-increasing bills. Everything has soared in the past few years. I always liked the story of the farmer who was accosted by the local feed merchant for not paying his bill, to which the farmer replied, 'When the bills come in at the beginning of the month I put them in the waste paper basket, gie them a bit steer, flick oot the top six and pay them. If *you're* no careful yours won't even get into the basket'.

February

As I trudged back through the snow, after feeding our Highland ponies this morning, and admiring Bonnie Strathearn in its white winter mantle and the sun just touching the top of Ben Vorlich, my thoughts were suddenly jarred by the squeak of a heron which my spaniel flushed from the wood burn. Its flight reminded my of that brilliant trilogy about the Cameron family in the eighteenth century. They were *The Flight of the Heron, The Gleam in the North*, and *The Dark Mile*. They were by D J Broster. In the first book, the flight of the heron was made out to be bad news for the beholder. So far as I was concerned could it be that the flight of the heron means the Tax man is going to come to me again for something. He seems to have an insatiable appetite. Or was the heron telling me that farming, still my ruling passion, is in for yet another battering. Just on Sunday night there was a programme on TV called 'You Are What You Eat' and the merits of that ghastly non-cholesterol margarine were extolled yet again against butter. Why has the country become obsessed with telling people what they should eat and drink in case one or two more die of a heart attack? I was always led to believe that heart disease was basically hereditary, but obviously according to the food fanatics I've 'got it wrong again, Dad'! No one warned myself and my pals when we volunteered to go to the war that some of us would not come back and some would be maimed. Funny how life was expendable then, but not now.

What I'm driving at is that we in the farming industry must fight back and fight back hard or else we'll land up trying to grow nothing but salad crops,and with Spain and Portugal now in the EEC we'd be on a hiding to nothing.

We have all to be good wee conservationists in future. What annoys me more than anything is that apart from a very small minority, we farmers are the best conservationists the Country has and it's infuriating that the average city dweller should think otherwise. That heron was maybe warning us that we are in for a tough time in agriculture as the 'antis' get more vociferous, the eating habits of the masses change, less is being spent on food and alternative crops become harder to find. Or maybe that heron was just saying Ben, now you're pensioned off you can't afford your dram! Perish the thought.

I have an old brazier in which I burn my bumph. This increased dramatically when I became a District Councillor. The brazier was made by a local Crieff blacksmith over forty years ago in the days when things were made to last and it was ordered by the late Duncan Stewart for heating branding irons, not for numbering lambs' horns as one would think, but for marking Highland heifers and cows that were unregistered but were thought suitable by members of the Society's Council for upgrading. There is no doubt at all that during the existence of that Scheme some animals with Shorthorn blood in their veins were passed and they did nothing but good to the breed as the 'hair and horns' enthusiasts were just about to ruin the breed's beef potential and also their hardiness. The cattlemen went to any lengths to have long trailing coats that all too often went with an unthrifty animal which sometimes still had on its winter coat at the Highland Show.

Bull stirks being prepared for the Oban sales used to be perched up on slatted pallets lest they lay in their wash and their heads were tied to each side lest they scratched themselves. It was almost a job for the RSPCA. But, luckily for the breed, Duncan Stewart came on the scene just after the war and brought all his stockmanship and his knowledge of Breed Society matters; having been a highly respected Council member of the Shorthorn Society and extremely knowledgeable on pedigrees. It was he who investigated the upgrading Scheme and I well remember going up to Ben More, Crainlarich, with him to upgrade heifers for a certain Miss Judy Crabbe, now Mrs. Judy Bowser - and look at the successes she has achieved since.

Duncans' stock bull at the time was a bull called Fearacher of Gartlea which had a white tail, a wee sign of a touch of Shorthorn, and with much more flesh and less hair than the fashionable bulls of that time. He and 'Ian of Glenfalloch' that followed him in the Fordie Fold had a terrific beneficial effect on the breed and there was a period in the early 'fifties when there was a Fordie bull in all the top folds in Scotland. Look at the success the breed is having today.

These thoughts were, of course, prompted by a rumour that the Aberdeen Angus were thinking of having an upgrading register. Bob Adam suggested just that some years ago when I took on as the breed's secretary and I backed him but the idea was turned down flat. When I see some of the bad hind legs and lack of backsides on some of the Canadian imports I wish we had done some more upgrading properly monitored at the time.

I had the rare distinction of being shown a small byre of Aberdeen Angus cows at Harviestown by that doyen of breeders J E Kerr. Everyone of them had great patches of white on them. In fact one of them could have passed as a belted Galloway. But they were real cows, heads on them like a housemaid and backsides like a cook.

In spring a young man's fancy turns to love, or so they say. As for me, 'my memory's fair awa' and I can't remember that long ago but now as an oldie in winter my fancy turns to welcoming the return of the sun on the few occasions that we see it. We have been kindly given permission to out-winter our Highland Ponies on a bit of Innerpeffray Moor, where they have always been, and in 22 years I have never seen it in such a 'sauce'. When I was a boy they used to talk about 'saucin' aboot wi' the kye' but this year its been 'saucin' aboot wi' the ponies'.

February

Perhaps it was because of this that I was desperately envious of a friend who returned from a trip to study agriculture in Israel. He is Robin Valentine, formerly of the now defunct 'Farming News' and he called his trip 'Israel Land of Milk, Honey and Quotas'.

The Quotas there, believe it or not, are on water of all things. Their agricultural outfit is fantastic for a country that is only the size of Wales as it earns three quarters of a billion dollars in foreign currency. Because their country runs from the Mediterranean up to skiing country and from desert to land 400 metres below sea level they can only cultivate 20% of it. But their Agricultural Research Departments are fantastic and should be a lesson to our Government who seem to want to jettison ours whenever the going for farming gets tough. Just the time when we need research. I don't see us changing to their Kibbutz system of which they have 270 (these are collective villages) where the people don't receive wages but get free housing, furniture, clothing, all meals and some pocket money; but their Moshav farms, of which there are 500, employing some 130,000 people, have a lot to commend them.

These are family co-operative holdings where every family owns 5 acres and one tractor and they share a pool of machinery. These people made a new start as migrants from 102 different countries and were overjoyed to be able to farm their own land and to be free. But it's their varied output that amazes me. Winter vegetables under plastic, goose livers for paté produced by Hungarian immigrants, cut flowers by Indian settlers. Avocados, peaches in pots 300 meters below sea level. Grapes on the Golan heights, strawberries under plastic, tomatoes in the winter months for top prices. They even breed ostriches which sell at £2,000 each!

Oh! I know all these crops need the sun but it's the country's ability to change their crops to suit world markets that is their secret to success and where we fail so sadly.

As I came back from Argyll where I'd been making a speech at a show dinner the heavens opened as only they can in that county and I realised not for the first time that we don't need water quotas. And I still wouldn't swap 'Caledonia stern and wild'for a thousand Israeli ostriches.

February

During the past fortnight I have had two days which I can only describe as out of this world.

The first was a case of 'Westering home with a song in the air' as I was going west to speak in Oban and the following night in Mull. As I headed west on the road from Crieff to Oban, on a road that I know like the back of my hand, I have never seen the scenery more lovely as the sun was setting firstly over Loch Awe and then further west over Oban Bay and Mull.

My toast was 'the land we live in'. What a super subject. It comes more easily to me than 'the Immortal Memory' which was my subject the next night. The views on the way over strengthened my belief that we live in the loveliest country of the world. I've seen a fair cross section of the world - fourteen countries to be exact.

Replying to my toast was John MacKay, our Under Secretary for agriculture, who like all politicians couldn't leave off Politics and he was naturally cock-a-hoop that his government had landed a big fish in the form of the Finnish Pulp Mill at Irvine. I told him afterwards how pleased I was about the much needed jobs for Scotland but added that I hoped that the mill would clear those thousands and thousands of acres in Scotland of unsightly Sitka spruce monstrosities and when they were replanted I hoped that some imagination would be used.

Then it was on to Mull and a Burns Night in the village. What fun I've had over the years in village halls and how I regret their passing.

The small committee for the measly sum of four pounds a ticket gave the locals an evening of first-class entertainment (bar my speech), plus a first-class meal and two free drams! It just shows what can be done with some enthusiasm.

Naturally I had to do some farming when I was there and was particularly interested in the island's Heifer retention scheme whereby farmers are paid to breed beef heifers if they are in calf to a bull of certain recognised beef breeds. I feel the Department slipped up badly here. If they had only laid down that the heifers had to be Highland, Galloway, Luing and Highland

February

Blue Grey Galloways, Irish Blue Greys yes and Hereford and Friesian in certain areas they would have had a more uniform cow stock instead of the collection of Heinz 57 varieties!

My other day out of this world was last Saturday, a day of brilliant sunshine, a nip in the air, and scarce a breath of air. I was sitting with my friend 2,300 feet above sea level, after a wee knobber stag had spoilt our excellent stalk on some hinds. We agreed as we looked at the breathtaking views that we wouldn't swap with anyone. And an added joy was seeing his ewes looking extra fit and grazing well above us demonstrating that hand feeding isn't always necessary with a good breeding policy plus good management which in his case included wise heather burning. But every picture tells a story. On Sunday I was going a bit short in my step and it was obvious I was over the allocated span and am living on borrowed time. Ah me!

"Only Fools and Horses", the TV show, is very funny. Many people in this neck of the woods thought my immediate neighbour Sandy Haggart either a fool or a horse when he bought four Aberdeen-Angus females nine years ago. It was well known that like all small farmers he was having a rough time. But still owning only four cows, he certainly put gossips' gas at a peep when at Perth Bull sales this year he topped the sale with a heifer at 5,200 gns and three bulls that averaged 1,800 gns! Not bad for a David in among the Goliaths. I always like it when some of the breeders with small herds and little financial backing come out and beat the big guns. But we need the big guns as well and during the past 40 years at Perth I've seen British Oxygen, Marks & Spencer, Littlewoods, different whisky firms etc, etc spend money on setting up herds in various breeds and different parts of the country. They all need stockmen. Invariably, they turn to Scotland for one, and where better? So often they buy Scottish stock as we are renowned for producing the best irrespective of breed. Just after the last war, when new methods of feeding livestock and especially show cattle were being introduced, there was a saying 'It would be a sad day when the art of the feeder took over from the art of the breeder'. Looking at the different breeds in Perth I just wondered.

An old pal of mine 'phoned up the other day in great agitation saying that every other sector of the farming industry was being subsidised but after

15

April 1st the beef industry would be on its backside with no variable premium. Judging by the trade for all good bulls at Perth the commercial breeders don't agree with him as I thought it a really sound trade and even the breed society secretaries seemed pleased. Surely, when the difference can be from 149p per kilo for a really quality prime animal down to 86p a kilo for a bad 'un, as it was on the Monday prime cattle sale in Perth on bull sale week, it must mean that quality beef *is* going to be needed even more, when we are being good boys and not using hormones. And that tasteless chicken might have been a cannibal, or might even have salmonella!

We've all got to put our house in order and go for quality. And talking of quality, pure Galloway and Highland beef are much in demand. I'll be off to Oban for the Highland sale where a large crowd is expected, but although tourism is its main means of employment nearly all the hotels will be shut. A past President of the Highland Cattle Society said 'Oban's a funny place, but we like it' and so do I.

It is now more than forty years since the bulls at the Perth Sales were paraded in Caledonian Road or 'on the street' as the late Connie McKenzie called it. That was in 1947, the year of the *real* storm and the street had to be cleared three times during the Aberdeen-Angus judging! It's high time the judging took place 'on the street' once more, and why? Because in those days Caledonian Road was a cobbled street and if you want to see how a beast walks, get it in the cobbles. Ninety per cent of the bulls at Perth would be like cats on hot bricks if they were walked on cobbles today and I'm sad to say that my old love the Aberdeen-Angus were among the worst offenders.

The Aberdeen-Angus Society has now agreed to a grading-up register. If only they had started it years ago. Better by far to have had a controlled grading-up scheme than the hoofs, tail heads and hind legs on all too many cattle that to me remind me of another breed completely alien to the Angus. It looks as if some beast somewhere didn't know who its father was, just like some bulls in all breeds by their colossal weights look as if they got lost in the rushes before they were registered!

There were three really good pronouncements at the Bull Sales. The first by Neil Massie, the new Angus President extolling his breeders for closer liaison with the commercial breeder and the family butcher who was the

one who really wants quality beef. And this was more than borne out by a country butcher on TV's 'Landward' - he wants a bit of fat on his carcases and has improved his business four fold as a result.

Then there was the good common sense from Bob Vigus, the Simmental breeder who said that we were trying to pack too much weight onto young bones that couldn't stand up to it and too many bulls were breaking down before the sales or were unable to work when they were bought and taken to their new home. We've all heard it so often privately but it's good to hear it brought into the open. Finally, that great old war horse, Alastair McKay, retiring after nineteen years as secretary of the Charolais Society and always wonderfully controversial: he made the true pronouncement that the art of the breeder would always beat that of the scientist. Hear, Hear, Alastair, we always did see eye to eye and agreed that, as proved so often at Smithfield, the Aberdeen-Angus and Charolais complement each other like gin and tonic.

Well the weather must be the main topic of everyone's conversation these days and especially farmers. The weathermen are likening February to that of 1947, but so far as we, in Strathearn, are concerned we haven't half the snow that we had in '47 and My, how the snow-clearing equipment has improved over the years.

At the end of last week I was listening and watching every weather forecast as the dread day had arrived, we were to flit from the farmhouse to our retiral cottage on the farm moor. Unlike my flitting from Gaskbeg to Ardlinglas, back in '59, when a well known firm of furniture removers tipped my furniture into a peat bog, between Spean and Roybridge (some things never to be recovered!). This time we did DIY with our friends and neighbours, and what fun it all was, on a lovely sunny day, but with a crisp air and the hills looking wonderful with their mantle of snow.

One sideboard, bought back in the 'fifties at a farm roup for under 100 notes was too big for the cottage so we had an antique dealer come to bid us for it. Imagine my delight when he said it was worth a grand!! I never struck a bargain so quickly in my life and as we'll have to build a car port the money is going to come in handy. At last inflation has done me some good!

After the Flitting all sorts of things came to light, the First volume of the Highland Cattle Society Herd Book of 1884 when their office was in Inverness. The then Earl of Breadalbane had one of the leading folds of that period and he of course was the one of whom it was written 'from Kenmore to Ben More the land is a' the Marquis's'. The Ben More being the one in Mull, of course so what a tract of country!. How sad that it was all squandered. Ben Challum and Blackmount Estates, that I managed at different times, were originally Breadalbane's. The herd book had a complete description of what the perfect Highland beast should look like with, as one would imagine, tremendous emphasis on the head, horn and hair but no mention of the fleshing qualities.

Then my 1955 Gaskbeg diary came to light with the acreages we were spraying for other farms, as we had the first sprayer in Upper Speyside and went as far as Boat of Garten and Carrbridge and the charge was 30 shillings per acre including the spray (it would hardly pay the diesel today). Well it's all over now and we're surrounded with boxes and I can't find anything that I need but Oh! the bliss of central heating (which it has taken me 70 years to purchase) and my next flitting will be to the crematorium which will no be my hassle!

March

Well, here we are into March and whatever the weather has in store for us we in Scotland have had a truly remarkable winter. A good friend of mine and one of my few listening fans once pulled my leg about broadcasting about 'wee birdies' as he called them on my moor. He isn't as old as I am and I love seeing the 'Peesies' and the oyster catchers come back inland again because to me they are the 'harbingers of Spring' and as one gets older one suffers more from the cold and damp and one longs for the first promise of spring with its snowdrops and the birds' spring migration.

Farming-wise, after a month of inactivity it's just great to see the ploughs once more in action.

My goodness! what an acreage those reversible ploughs can blacken in a day - some 10 acres I suppose if the going is good in this area where most fields will average just that, and using a three furrow plough. How different from the horse days when an acre a day was considered a good day's work but we always got the seed in and we always had a harvest and there were jobs galore and we didn't have grain mountains and we were happy with our lot.

Changed days I fear when money has become the be all and end all of life, not job satisfaction. Talking of those horse days I was so glad to see that the Buchlyvie 150th ploughing match was at last able to be held after having waited a month since it was originally meant to take place and there were ten pairs of horses entered. I know there is no way the horse will ever come back into his own (although the so called light-legged variety have just about taken over every agricultural show in the country) but there could well be a place for the 'orra baste' for odd jobs and feeding stock as the price of tractors goes through the roof and north sea oil comes to an end. At least a horse can be fed off the farm. I passed a ploughman making a lovely job with a reversible plough but I did notice three or four stobs leaning at a 45 degree angle where the plough had hit them and it made me think what a long end rigg one has to leave with those modern juggernauts!

I had Highland ponies running in a stubble field here that was due to be ploughed and by the time I got back from a Council meeting the field was black ground and the ponies were moving over the field eating the newly turned up earth. All stockmen worth their salt know that if a beast is not eating properly, and especially in the case of prize cattle who have been on a high plane of nutrition, earth from a mole hill sets their stomachs right.

March

There was the famous story told about two of our best-known Scottish stockmen at Smithfield, (both having won the overall championship at one time or another). They had a beast that wasn't cudding so they turned on their young unsuspecting apprentices, gave them a graip apiece, and said get us some earth. Can you imagine the laddies' thoughts and feelings as they sallied forth into the concrete jungle that surrounds Earls Court. History relates that being good Scots, with the Scots' unusual initiative, they decided to look for a graveyard which they found after being chased out of two gardens, on one occasion by a fierce guard dog. The upshot was the beast got better.

Last week I had a most enjoyable day out at one of our local livestock markets when they were selling their fatstock. The camaraderie and the crack was guid and one farmer showed me his line on which I saw Blackfaced lambs at £35 and there would be some sub to draw. These lambs could be bought £25/£27 in the backend so the finisher is getting a useful and much needed return after last summer's disastrous harvest. Another pal showed me his cattle line and it was a very different story with beasts making but a fraction over their buying-in price 'but I've got their dung and had the pleasure of their company' he philosophically said. Farms that use a lot of dung certainly stand out in this area compared with the 'dust ranches' but it would take someone much more able than I am to forecast where beef is going, what with the beef mountains, this anti-fat lobby, cost of production etc, etc.

During the flitting, which seems to go on and on (Oh! how I'm missing the sheds and out houses at the steading), I had the dog kennel moved. It was made in 1947 by a local Crieff joiner, whose sons now make forklift trucks. That kennel went from Millhills to Gaskbeg, then to Ardkinglas, next to Woodburn Farm and now its last resting place will be here. I remember the joiner telling me at the time that I was lucky as it was made from some imported Canadian timber that he had. I'm sure the unseasoned rubbish we use today won't be so durable, but then the whole policy of our country nowadays is that nothing should last.

March

The rabbits this spring have had a bonanza on the tree barks. I've never seen so much damage, even the 20 year-old apple and plum trees up at the farm are completely 'stripped', as are my new ones down at the cottage which of course in hindsight I should have covered. As the winter was not as severe as many could the lack of sunshine last summer have had something to do with it? Some farmers at the market were complaining that although they had plenty of lambs all too many didn't have the will to live. Could this also be lack of sun on the ewes last year or on the hay or the silage? If it is, one thing is certain, there won't be enough spare cash around this year for farmers to fly off to seek the sun.

I was saddened to hear of the death of that great old warhorse of farming journalism, John Cherrington. Although we seldom saw eye to eye with each other we each had a mutual respect for the other, and our opinions, as we both started our careers in the hard times of the 1930s, he in New Zealand, and I in the Borders and Sussex, but both with a love of sheep. John couldn't stand the razmatazz of the show ring whereas I thrive on it. I remember when he was interviewing me in one of the first farming TV shows (so long ago that it was from Alexandra Palace). John was as usual denigrating all shows, I slipped the red rosette out of my coat that I had won with my

Highland bullock that day at Smithfield and said 'John, your trouble is you've never won one of these'. End of argument.

Another time we were on a radio farming link-up and the subject was the future of organic farming (which in those far-off days we called 'Muck and Magic'). I was reminded of that broadcast this week when Sally and I tasted some of the sweetest carrots we've eaten for many a long day. It transpired that these were grown by a local farmer who has decided that because his farm is no longer viable he must specialise in organic crops. All power to his elbow say I as I never was a great lover of nitrogen. Oh! I know it worked wonders for us in the years that we were asked to expand our production but all too many have thought that if X amount was the prescribed dose then X plus 2 would give double the crop, only to be faced with a laying crop and extra nitrogen seeping into the burns.

I remember once growing a crop of oats at Woodburn without enough nitrogen, before I got the farm into good heart. It didn't pay me, but it could be a different story today as at last the oat growers are getting their just reward. I support their rise in popularity, it is due to the amount of horse keepers (and copers) that there are and also to the new generation of muesli eating yuppies. I only hope that too many don't jump on the oat growing band waggon as it could muck up the price but their lateness in ripening with the advent of the combine has put a lot of farmers against growing them. Why oh why so many farmers sow them last, not first, of their spring crops simple defeats me.

Another sign of the times this last fortnight was a well-known Scottish supermarket banning sales of fig products which might contain any unwanted additives. We the farming industry have been slow to move with the consuming public's wishes, fickle though they may be. As for me, I don't give a fig for what Edwina Currie says and I just love my beef with a bit of fat on it and lashings of home made butter. I have at least 2 eggs every morning, all scrumptious.

How I hate March with its biting East winds that rip my liver to shreds (or that's what I blame at least). And then this year we had the 'fill dyke' not in February but last week followed by a virtual tornado. The cold and the wet just made me wonder how the spring corn, that some optimists were sowing the week before the storm, would be feeling now. I was always an April sowing man myself but of course in the old days we weren't as 'far forrit wi the work' as they are today and I suppose shortage of labour must inevitably push one on. But around this district although the light ground was drying on the top it was desperately cold and wet underneath.

But let's talk of something cheerier. Soon April and spring must be on its way as the peewits, oyster catchers and my favourites, the whaups, wheel and cry out their individual spring songs that lift an old man's heart and give him the promise of spring that he looks forward to more each year that passes. On TV last Sunday we saw the 'Landward' team enjoying themselves at the first of the National Shows, the one in Paris. I know only too well that it's not all oysters and Chablis: the first year I went there with Aberdeen-Angus cattle and a steak bar the former were in the furthest away cattle hall and the latter in the food hall and it took me three quarters of an hour to get from one to the other on a crowded Sunday. In those days the rings were sawdusted and, with one thing and another, I came home with no voice. Sally thought I had been up to no good and came out the following year but she also succumbed to the throat soreness and left me to go it alone in succeeding years. But for all the hard work we put in we never made a dent in the French market as they are fiercely defensive of their own products. I was glad to hear Billy Hogg was importing Normandy cattle, always my favourites, a true dual purpose breed but one I was told had to live near the English Channel! Then this last fortnight the planting Glenlednock Forestry wrangle burst out again when the Estate who want to plant organised a showing of their plans which drew 150 people, mostly 'antis'; the next night the anti-planners held their own packed meeting. There is no doubt this will be a test case and may well have repercussions for all would-be agro-foresters. As usual the estate factor was left to explain the plan. I'm not anti-landlord, for the Highlands have had millions poured into them from money made elsewhere but the factor, as I know (having factored 10 estates), is paid to do the dirty work.

As a young factor, I didn't know what to say to a fiery old head stalker whom I know was against my appointment so I said to him 'have you any problems with vermin, Dougie?' 'Aye,' he said, 'a puckle hoodie crows and a factor'. Nuff said.

March

A little nest in the countryside with roses at the front door seems to be every townee's idea of heaven. So far as the South East corner of Britain is concerned it is causing mayhem with the planning authorities and a packet to the townee who wants to build it. All planning authorities in Scotland are now being deluged with plans for more country cottages and as a councillor I'm finding it one of our hardest tasks. The big snag that I personally face each time is that I want people to live in the countryside because it's people that matter and without people the countryside dies. But, and it's a big but, where? Do we want to see cottages dotted higgledy-piggledy all over the place? Do we want to start new villages, or do we want to tack on to other small sets of buildings. For myself, I'm for the latter trying to form clachans out of existing small numbers of communities. But the real snag comes when one sees the types of houses that are being built today. Because of expense 99 per cent are kit-type bungalows and some can be extremely tasteful: we have one in this parish that blends into the countryside as if it had been there for a century. But all too many are for all the world like blown-up match boxes and completely alien to the surrounding environment. This is where we farmers and landowners come in. Some old-fashioned steadings that already blend so well into their background are ripe for development and we have one or two in our district that are a joy to behold now that they have been completed.

The Government wishes land taken out of production and used for more houses, trees, areas of recreation or scenic areas. In Perth & Kinross District we have had what could be a test case so far as planting trees is concerned. The landlords wanted to plant 150 acres of a particularly lovely area, Glenlednock. Naturally there was tremendous local opposition, extremely well organised, urging our council to refuse permission to plant. This they did by 17 votes to 10. I had moved the amendment that the poorer land, roughly about two thirds of the area should be planted leaving the spectacular view unspoiled and also the downfall land untouched. The decision could be overthrown by the Forestry Commission who would still OK the grant, in this case £75,000. It seems to me there is something far wrong somewhere, and with farming in the doldrums I can see an awful lot of forestry planning applications in the pipeline which will have to be dealt with sympathetically.

March

It's thirty one years since I was President of the Highland Cattle Society and I was delighted to be present this week at what I considered to be the best Bull sale I attended this year. The reason it was better than the Galloway sale was that the sound trade was made by home breeders not by Germans. The Germans are however buying Highland Cattle heavily and I only hope the breeders that have remained faithful to our oldest breed will not be tempted to sell their best heifers as that is the sure way to ruin a good fold.

At the March meeting of the Royal Smithfield Club, one of our most respected ex-Presidents and celebrated Smithfield market wholesale butcher was heard to say that compared with our cattle in Scotland the South don't know the meaning of quality beef. How does one start to educate the modern '"fast food"' housewife about quality? I had a relation from London staying with us and I got her to taste a Golden Wonder tattie - about which she was ecstatic. But when she saw them first she said 'you'd never sell these in London, their eyes are far too deep and everyone shopping in supermarkets wants potatoes that have no eyes and are scrubbed'. Well there's an old Scottish saying 'You canna Hae Baith'.

The Smithfield Club visited the Moredun Institute. Every time I go I learn about some new project on which they've embarked. The Barnes Review has recommended a swingeing cut of 20% in their grant saying that their 'near market' research should be covered by the agricultural industry and commercial companies. What a lot of old codswallop! How can our already beleaguered industry get a further £2.6 million, because that's the figure that's being cut; or would a pharmaceutical company back research that is 'nearly marketable' if some of that research proved that the commercial company's claims for its product were not what they've cracked it up to be.

As someone very interested in Red Deer, I was riveted to hear how very real the TB threat is in that species, thanks to an importation from Hungary to a herd that has been dispersed widely. It will have to be closely monitored. It seems that the TB test that we all know so well had, because of the deer's very thin skin, to be meticulously carried out and I fear that one vet whom I knew 50 years ago wouldn't get away with sticking the syringes in anywhere and coming back two days later rubbing his hand down the beast's neck saying 'she's fine!'

The really stupid thing about the Barnes Review cut on Moredun is that the Institute is doing so much research that benefits humans. Long before 'the hysteria' it was doing research on listeria and salmonella. When we got to the area where the salmonella was being researched there was an empty chair and when told the lady was absent and not too well I was prompted to ask 'was her name Currie?'

I often wonder what people who are not farmers do when travelling by train. For me, I mentally farm other people's farms for the whole journey, sometimes applauding, sometimes criticising. My most recent journey was to Preston in Lancashire and I was amazed at the amount of winter cereals I saw in what used to be a predominantly dairying area. No wonder we have a surplus of cereals or have we? Judging by the reports of the droughts in America, the real bread basket of the world, we could yet see those who jumped up and down and railed against the 'fat cats' of the farming world, having to eat their words.

Another thing that struck me was the number of corners of fields that were fenced off and had been planted with I take it hard woods judging by the amount of grow cones, a first class invention. Going down the West coast route, where it has been very wet, I saw all too much laying water and I fear me that one of the victims of the farming recession will be drainage, so essential to good farming practice. My reason for travelling to Preston was to do a 'voice over' to a T V video made in the summer for the Highland Cattle Society in preparation for the British Food and Farming Year Jamboree in Hyde Park in May.

The Highland Cattle Society have got so many new members and breeders that it was felt that a video explaining the management of a Highland Fold could do nothing but good and when translated would be more than useful for the many many overseas breeders who have recently bought cattle. I must say it does my heart good to see a reversal of the craze for importing each and every overseas breed that 'get rich quick entrepreneurs' fancy, and now the two oldest breeds, the Highlanders and Galloways, discarded for so long, are leading the way in the exporting boom.

The night before I went to Preston I had been in the Borders speaking to their Area NFU dinner and came away wondering why more NFU areas don't go in for one good slap-up show and doing away with the half dozen

March

or so Branch dinners. It certainly in the past would have given me more nights in my own bed instead of hotel ones where the beds are always too short for me!

During the day I was on a farm beside the real Preston, the one in Berwickshire, and there they were sowing lime and the tractor wasn't even making a mark and the farmer said he could have sown corn but he feared for a late frost. What a difference from us here, up to our knees in glaur!

As I sat in Elie, Fife last week overlooking the lovely bay, I watched some wind surfers who were masters of their craft (literally). What worried me is how on a weekday did they have that time to spend. I met them later and it turned out that they had nothing they would rather do. One of them made the surf boats for a living as he found there were more and more people with time on their hands.

What on earth has this to do with farming, you may ask? A damned lot say I as farming gets a tougher row to hoe and if the farm workers continue to ask for stupid rises of £50 per week then more of the industry will be turning to leisure pursuits either to make money out of them or because they haven't a job and will spend more time in leisure. We are finding on our District Council that our Leisure & Recreation Committee is asking for a larger share of the financial cake for nice looking public parks, playing fields, rights of way etc, etc.

Going back to the farm workers and their demands, I have always been a tremendous supporter of this and always felt that in the good post war years too many farmers didn't pass on enough of their benefits to their men. I never thought a man who was on the minimum wage was worth employing and always gave over the odds to a good yin, if not in money then in perks. But times have changed and there are contractors (with a lot of money tied up in machinery) willing to go long distances for work.

Farmers' sons, too, are doing a lot of contracting work for their neighbours. I've been thinking of many families with whom I have neighboured over the past forty years and how lucky we are in farming that this still exists. How would sheep have been gathered off our vast expanse of Highland hills without the neighbours. Contractors have come in there too, but they don't know the ground as do neighbours or the lug marks when one is mothering up the straggler lambs on a marking day. And on arable farms how super to see neighbours share their equipment, or help finish a belated harvest.

When I was a laddie and worked for a rich farmer in Norfolk I was shocked when he charged his neighbour for the loan of some old horse machinery and these were the really hungry late 1920s and early '30s. We had to touch our forelocks - for me, a laddie, half a crown a week - when we got our pay. Could it be a coincidence that the farm workers' union started in that neck of the woods?

April

'The Cradle of Champions', Jim Morton (late of Farmer and Stockbreeder) once called Strathspey when he was up doing a piece for his paper back in 1957, the year after I'd bred 'Highland Princess' which won the Scottish National and Smithfield overall Championships. I was only following in the footsteps of countless others, for Speyside at one time was peak among the areas that bred fat stock cattle.

They say you should never go back to your old haunts because of the changes that will have taken place but as the girls wanted a day or two skiing - and they got ideal conditions for it - I had time on my hands to ferret around an area which I dearly love. It was great to get the Highland hospiality welcome, (so sadly lacking in all too many hotels today) from my old friend Nigel in Grantown even though he has moved to another hostelry; it was marvellous to be hailed by my old friends the Doctor and his wife from Laggan, sadly the former losing his eyesight which may have been lucky for me as he thought I was looking very fit and, because of his failing eyesight, couldn't see my 'alcoholic glow'.

But as always it was the change in the farming that I really wanted to see. The only things that hadn't changed were the amount of mole hills. From Laggan to Grantown was one sea of mole hills and there is a fortune to be made by a good 'moudie' trapper or perhaps when the grass farmers think they are increasing their acreage as the heaps take up more space than the flat. There were nothing like the old number of Blackface wintering ewe hoggs as more farmers have gone in for their own flock and those that I saw certainly wouldn't be wintered for five shillings and threepence for a head - which was the price we used to pay back in the 'forties! The two radical changes were the amount of new buildings (most of them very ugly) and the general use of silage. When I went to Gaskbeg in 1951 and made silage I was laughed to scorn but now everyone is at it and how much easier it is to make with modern machinery and technical knowledge. No longer does everything get sticky with treacle nor is the weekend spent worrying whether the pit is going to overheat. Nowadays it is very straightforward and just recently a 'silascope' has been invented which will tell the farmer whether or not an additive is required and how much. With the dicey and delighted future for beef I was surprised to see the large numbers of suckler cows in the Strath, and the ease of making silage must have a large bearing on the increase. But oh dear what a mixture of breeds! Gone are the days when only two breeds, the Shorthorn and Angus, were used (and we all know the reason for their demise) but I certainly wouldn't like to pick replacement heifers from 90% of the herds I saw. As I nearly bought Cuil but couldn't get a bank to back me all those years ago (changed days) a look at Cuil and Dalchully was a Must.

I was amazed that one of the ITV channels made a programme on the legendary Mr Herbage when all those of us who had farmed in the Highlands for years were told that we weren't making use of the water, the peat, the stones etc and that a pedigree herd of Ayrshires and Aberdeen Angus and a Highland Fold were being set up.

Well in my half century in farming I can count on one hand people who have made money out of pedigree cattle. And when it comes to Laggan, where I farmed for eight years, you have a seven month winter. So it came as no great surprise to me that on the very night that I had shown Sally Dalchully and Cuil land - from the car of course - the news broke that Mr H had to find £400 million in debts. I must say if you're going to go broke make a right job of it but it's mighty tough on the creditors, especially local labour.

And of course no visit to Speyside would be complete without a visit to Jimmie Gordon, now 88. Some young farmers and NFU delegates who think they can debate should have attended the Strathspey farmers' discussion group in the 'fifties and heard Jimmie, the late Donald Allan Ballintomb and the late George Stokes getting at each other's throats. That was debating at its best. I remember one debate on having a trade mark put on all Scottish Beef and Lamb. There's nothing new in this world!

In some parts of Scotland we've been having more than our fair share of rain. Now the drying east winds have arrived. I had reason to go through the Carse of Stirling last week and farm after farm had bings of large fertiliser bags in their yards as there was no way their heavy soil could take a tractor.

As I passed through I thought of the many halycon days on school holidays that I had helped stack Timothy hay for which the Carse is famous. These were the days of huge stacks and the hay being lifted from the ground by a

big grab which was pulled up by a rope on a pulley with the horse power being just that - usually the oldest and quietest horse on the farm and looked after by this wee laddie! Why is it that in my ageing mind every day then seemed to be sunny or is my memory 'fair awa'? When one thinks that the Carse, which is so productive, was hand made before mechanisation, it's mind-boggling. Originally it was covered in peat feet deep and the first tillers of that soil cut the peat off and dumped it in the Forth to unearth the highly productive heavy soil which is famous for its production of Timothy hay and wheat. When I was in Sussex, before the war there was in the Estate on which I worked a mixture of chalk and heavy land. The old farm manager was adamant that stock should never be left on the heavy fields; if we had a wet autumn in Carse the fields were poached. His argument was that the old ponds in that country - and there were many - were made by cattle compacting the soil in a hollow and the rain just filling them in. Judging by the pools I've seen this spring which I have never seen before, something is far wrong. My own belief is that a lot of our drainage systems were put in for the horse era and   managed to stand up to the wee grey Ferguson tractors and some of the other smaller models but no way can those old systems stand up to these modern Goliaths that seem to be all the rage today. I was delighted to hear a soil scientist echo these sentiments last week as this had been a hobby horse of mine for many years.

April

When I was up in Gaskbeg in Inverness-shire, all those thirty years ago, the weather men were nowhere near as accurate as they are today and I used to get really fizzing when we were told that the weather was wonderful and the outlook was set fair while we at 1,000 ft above sea level were under a foot of snow.

I had much the same feelings last Friday when I heard it said on the radio that the spring cereals were all sown - and we in this Strath hadn't made a start. It's the old story, that wonderful 'Golden Ring' that stretches up the eastern seaboard from Berwick-on-Tweed north has always had the best of it and always will. That's why in the past so many farming families who were knocking their guts out on a wet Ayrshire or Lanarkshire farm (milking cows seven days a week and by hand of course) moved over to the East and did very well.

When factoring Blackmount I was asked to chair the local Deer Management Group. This Group consists of Glen Lyon, Glen Lochay, Glen Dochart and the area of Blackmount east of the Bridge of Orchy-Fort William railway. The object of the Group is to find out, by taking an annual census, or count in the spring, and then deducting the cull numbers how we stand with regard to total numbers. The interesting thing is that since the price of venison rose dramatically we in our Group find we have been shooting too many stags and not enough hinds. Poaching, too, has been on the increase: it's no longer 'one for the pot' but £80 plus in notes from an unscrupulous hotelier or butcher (if there is such a thing!). At our meeting last week, where they very kindly asked me to continue as Chairman, not everyone was disappointed that venison had slumped by some 30p per lb. It may sort out some Deer Forest owners' problems.

Just as 'Meadow Lamb is the fatter but Mountain Lamb is sweeter', give me a yeld hind, well hung, which has grazed a heather hill, rather than venison from a young farmed beast. Venison, like herring, is wholesome fairing and more should be eaten.

My mother, now nearing 99 and still enjoying her Gin and tonic, has a marvellous saying when things are not going to her liking. She says 'The Lord moves in a mysterious way his Blunders to perform'. With three weeks of rain, cold winds, and sodden fields and no grain around here sown for the past three weeks, many arable farmers will be echoing her sentiments. We always reckoned in the old days that every day delayed sowing after the the 14th of April meant a bushel an acre shortfall in yield. But is the Lord being so daft? Maybe he is seeing to it that we don't have another bumper harvest and it was good to hear from Charlie Allan the other night that some of the grain mountain was at last beginning to move, albeit slowly. I've been reminding a moaning farmer that we were promised and always got a seed time and harvest and he rightly replied 'Aye, but the old man never said what the yield was to be'.

Judging by the articles in the countless farming journals that one receives these days, we are in for the same arguments about grain as we had about milk. Price restraint or quotas and of course with grain the possibility of a co-responsibility levy. Whatever is decided, we as a farming community have got to stop being a lot of ostriches and expect the EEC to stump up millions every year to support cereals.

Oh! listen to Ben preaching, it's all right for him, he's retired! True but I'm a fervent countryman and always have and always will be and if the whole industry doesn't take surpluses seriously we'll land up as they have in the States with farmers going to the wall, and it's always the wee men who go first. I've seem some of the thousands of acres in the States that were taken out of production and to a farmer's eye it's not a bonny sight. Better by far that we think of alternatives now.

If there's one thing I enjoy in life it's talking to a craftsman and watching him or her at their work, be it carpenter, artist, blacksmith or farmer. Yes, farmer. To my mind the farmers who are surviving in these awful times are *craftsmen*, are on top of their job and are able to ride out adversity such as we are going through just now.

Thanks to attending a spring show and sale of cattle ten days ago, I met an old friend who had just proved his craftsmanship by lifting both prizes for steers and heifers and when I questioned him about his farming system he invited me to go to see it. The sale itself was a flyer and as I hadn't attended one for a bit, I got the shock of my life. There didn't seem to be anything under £500. My old-fashioned idea of a fair price was 100 pence a kilo. Now it's more like 150 pence! We all know the old saying that 'there is a new crop of fools born every year when the grass grows'. Some of the ablest men in our industry are still buying cattle, but the amount they now have to invest is terrifying. As always, the best drawn and shown pens make the top prices, a sign of craftsmanship. When I went to see my friend's set-up, two things struck me. Firstly that he had stuck to breeding his own cattle and had some 250 breeding females about him which will be a deal more saleable than clapped-out machinery!

Secondly, in his carefully worked out breeding policy, using Simmental and Charolais, the old Scotch Beef Shorthorn was at the base of it. In case of losses at calving before the calving season he bought six calves from a known disease free source and had them on a nursette 'just for fear'. That's craftsmanship. His terminal sire was the Charolais and by his show and sale results 'the proof of the pudding is in the eating'. But he did admit he bought Aberdeen-Angus steaks himself, so how long will it be before he has the courage to give others what he eats himself. How sad that in this land world-famous for beef production so many Scottish farmers gave up their breeding herds because of a temporary recession.

Chopping and changing policy in farming has never paid off and although there was a period when cattle seemed only to leave the pleasure of their company as profit, what about the fertility they left?

My friend told me that thanks to his cattle his agronomist has cut the fertiliser bill by half, no mean saving these days. But the last word on this craftsman's set-up was when he bought his first Charolais bull and his old cattleman who had never fed anything but black cattle all his life, was heard to say to the grieve 'We're no needin' yin of' they brits, we're fully mechanised'.

Glamis church was packed when the farming fraternity gathered to pay homage to one of its greats, Bob Adam. The congregation read like a 'Who's Who' in the livestock breeding world. Far be it from me to give an obituary on this programme. I couldn't compete with the excellent one in the Scottish Farmer. But Bob was a big man and we had a wonderful love/hate relationship. He came to Woodburn each autumn to look over my suckled calves before they went to the calf sale at Killin and he had to be given venison of which he was desperately fond. He was a big man in every way and did things in a big way but he was extraordinarily humble for one who was a world respected figure. Why I said we had a love/hate relationship is that he just loved to make money and if it meant jettisoning the Aberdeen-Angus breed for the Charolais and then them for the Limousin, he was quite ruthless and he made money every time. As secretary of the Aberdeen-Angus Society, I was not amused and told him so and we had a real old ding dong row about it, but until his death, and I saw him more often and more recently than many of his fair weather friends, we remained great pals. Oh! I know some people said he bred his Angus too small and dumpy but as with all stockmen he bred for the market demand.

And of course, Bob like many another Scottish farmer made his original cash from seed potatoes. In the late 'Forties when at Millhills, there were two neighbouring railway stations, the Highlandman and Innerpeffray. What has that to do with potatoes? Just this, that an unscrupulous tattie merchant used to get the then Stock Seed Grade 'OK'd' at one station and then fill up waggons of the then 'H' Grade (which was damned near brock) at the other and then get waggons together in Crieff to be sent South as S S Seed. I am glad to say that, even allowing for the odd fraudulent merchant, the Scottish seed and tattie trade is still the great bastion of our farming industry in this Strath and many another. One of my neighbours tells me that he has just dressed out 210 tons, mostly Pentland Squire and some Desiree, and he only had two baskets of rotten tatties. Some achievement. He said he found he has done better using a bucket not an elevator to lift them to a height of 9 ft and of course he has ducts below. All I can say is, thank God they don't have to stand outside on these freezing mornings dressing them out of those outside pits covered in wheat straw and 'winter happed' forbye! Some things have improved for the better.

It's been great these last few weeks to see the tractors rushing up and down our country roads even although as an oldie I keep thinking their new yellow lights mean they are about to turn to the right.

I have been chappin on doors, electioneering. I have become an expert on the different types of letterboxes we have in this country. I hate the ones that have a bristly brush inside them through which one has to force the leaflet (which of course extols my dubious merits) and at one home where a ferocious dog was snarling, the leaflet was snatched out of my hand but luckily I saved my fingers (I should think the dog found the leaflet contents most indigestible!) At another I heard a hoover going in the hall and of course couldn't attract the lady but she suddenly burst out of the door asking me for another as the hoover had devoured the first!. That was infinitely better than the man who took one look at me and the leaflet, tore it up, threw it in my face and said 'Nothing but a lot of bloody rubbish'.

I represent the lovely Valley of the Almond which runs from the rich acres of Strathearn into the foothills of the Grampians. As you can imagine I love visiting and 'Ceilidhing' with the farmers, and the hill farmers especially, and one whom I have known for ages was enthusing about his success of in-wintering his blackie ewes. When I think of the raised eyebrows and scorn that was cast on me when I started in-wintering hoggs over 30 years ago, it's great to see how it has taken on. This farmer said to me that if his son wanted to take on the 1,800 ewes he had advised him to split the lambings so that the whole stock could be lambed inside. I was also very taken with the divisions he had in his shed which were a line of boxes with gates in front (next the lambing ewes) and behind an empty bit of the shed. As a ewe lambed she was popped into the box and once properly mothered was let out of the back, hence doing away with mismothering.

But the sad thing on my rounds was to see the ever increasing number of derelict farmhouses, steadings and cottages. Three have become empty in one small hill area since I canvassed there four years ago. How do we turn this overwhelming tide?

Then I had to see some 'braw calves' by a Black Bull and after spending at least twenty minutes admiring them I quietly asked if I could have the farmer's support at the election. To which the farmer said 'It's like this Ben, my faither aye voted Tory so I do too'. I'm sad that Politics are taking over in local Government.

I used to know a shepherd in Argyll who, whenever we had two successive dry days said 'We could do wi a wee bit shooer, Captain.' It would seem

April

that our grain expert is of the same mind as this week he said that those of you on light land were needing rain. So what! You'll get it as sure as God made little apples. For me, give me this past week of warmth. There's plenty of sap just under the top soil. It was on one of those gorgeous balmy mornings that I was making my leisurely way home from my annual spring foray to my beloved Border Country. I was travelling from Berwick-on-Tweed to Edinburgh, not on the A1 but via Paxton and Greenlaw and I thanked God for two reasons. Firstly for the sheer joy of being alive and being able to enjoy the sight of land well farmed, and secondly, I thanked him that I wasn't Minister of Agriculture who will eventually be the person who decides what diversification there will be for farmers. Looking at that beautifully farmed land how could one do anything else with it but farm it? The crops looked good, the stock looked in good nick, the hedges trimmed, the cottages perfect, the farmhouses and gardens well tended and enough coppices and woodlands for shelter and game cover without giving a blanket covering appearance. It was a joy to behold on that spring morning and the townsfolk who accuse farmers of bespoiling the country-side would do well to travel round Scotland before they criticise us. Now the South of England, that's another story!

I was present at a very happy occasion 10 days ago; it was the final turf being placed on a stone dyke by an Argyll Laird. The dyke was started two years ago when I factored the Estate and introduced a Feoga Grant Scheme in which one can claim 70% for the restoration of stone dykes. As one who started my farming on hill places, I realised only too well what the bield of a stone dyke means to stock.

I was extremely fortunate in the dyker I got and it was just great to see the finished article, a good 0.5 mile plus the fank.

The Laird in question had an antipathy to beards but changed his mind after he saw the job the bearded dyker and his bearded helpers made.

I remember a bearded dyker in father's congregation over 50 years ago, he was constructing a new dyke for an American woman who wore very thick pebble specs and he said to her 'Are you ittlin to have your dyke turf tappit?' To which the woman replied 'Whaat?' The dyker repeated 'Are you ittlin to have your dyke turf tappit?' Back came the same reply 'Whaat?' As she walked off the dyker straightened up and called after father 'Yon woman's deef as weel as blint'".

May

'Auld Ayr whom n'er a toon surpasses for honest men and bonny lasses!' So wrote Rabbie Burns, but for those of us in the farming world it is also famous for having the first Scottish county show of the season. Nothing I enjoy more than going to a show, through an area that I haven't seen for some time and farming other folks' land! Being nearer the Atlantic than Perthshire there were any amount of cattle that had been turned out to grass and they weren't travelling round and round the fields but were either 'tethered by their teeth' or were lying contentedly. An old farming friend of mine once told me many years ago 'Laddie you can't put your beasts out too early or house them early enough'. The latter was certainly true last back end when many a pasture was poached to bits.

How things have changed at our shows since the war. Of course the advent of overseas cattle and sheep breeds is a change that goes on and I wonder what breed some of our entrepreneurs are going to find next, from some unknown valley in Europe. I only hope that they are not freaks like one imported cattle breed that can hardly walk, have to be caesared to produce a calf, and have a life span of but a few summers compared with our natives. But I was thrilled to see an Aberdeen-Angus cow as the Champion of Champions, and a good cattle beast she was too.

Then there were the Ayrshires, and this was their 150th Quey Derby (a quey is a heifer or first calver). Ayrshires have such lovely female lines. Although South West Scotland was originally beef country the stockmen there made a first-class job of producing the Ayrshire breed, seen to perfection at their County Show.

Then there were the majestic Clydesdales which are having such a resurgence, even if not for farm work nowadays. No show in Scotland is complete without its Clydesdales. But of course every show is now full of what local show committees call 'light-legged horses' and Ayr had four rings full of them going hammer and tongs for two days.

On the trade stand side what a change to see all the banks now present. Their job used to be to refuse loans, but more recently they have tried to shove money down our throats. Perhaps they are there to make sure that we are spending our overdrafts properly.

The snack bars are tremendously improved thanks to the voluntary organisations like 'Riding for the Disabled', 'Cancer Research', 'Heart Relief', etc. All with rolls and fresh fillings and good hot coffee. But why oh why are show lunches always similar and unappetising - packet soup, tough overdone beef, tasteless chicken, tinned veg, piles of chips and tinned fruit salad. I thought Ayr would have done better. We judges were fed in the Racecourse restaurant but there was no imagination and precious little fresh Scotch produce.

The other thing that hasn't changed is the love/hate relationship towards judges. I asked an old pal why he wasn't showing and he replied 'A' my judges are deid'.

I wonder with the high price of beef cattle today how many farmers realise how many of our youth are serious vegetarians and what that means for future generations of beef producers. I took my daughter out for lunch in her University town and there were no fewer that three vegetarian restaurants all packed with students. When she suggested one to her old Dad the reply was sharp and to the point 'No way! You were educated on beef!' Better than a friend of mine in the Carse of Stirling who said his boys were educated 'on Timothy Hay'.

Well I've seen it all now. A farming TV programme form England with a biologist at Cambridge University, highly paid I've no doubt, telling us farmers how he was monitoring stock behaviour. Have some of those boffins never heard of the word stockmanship? I remember as a callow youthful groom at Lavington Stud Sussex, when we turned the yearlings out to grass in the spring one groom stayed with them for a goodly while to see that a colt or a filly wasn't getting bullied. If it was it was taken out. And any cattleman worth his salt (and that means everyone I've been lucky enough to know) always moves any beast that is being 'hooleted' in the cattle court.

Townspeople get the impression that we farmers are cruel to animals for the sake of profit. In all sections of the community there are bound to be a few who put profit before animal contentment - and I for one don't like sow stalls, but would they reproduce and perform so well if they were really uncomfortable?

Then there was that lovely TV show 'Where Eagles Fly' with the most spectacular photography. Full marks to the photographer who was 20 ft from the Eyrie for two days on end - what patience *and* discomfort! But they spoilt it all by saying there were 400 pairs of eagles in the country and enough grouse for the shooting interests (worth millions of pounds per annum) *and* the eagles. A load of old codswallop say I. It's strange that an Estate I used to manage got 40 brace of grouse on the glorious twelfth when they had one pair of eagles and now they have four pair of eagles they get one brace of grouse. And as for eagles not taking lambs, well well! As if a bird of prey who can take, on the film's admission, something as well camouflaged as a deer calf would leave a lonely twin lamb which sticks out like a sore thumb. Don't get me wrong, I love eagles and have spent hour after hour lying in the heather admiring that wonderful, majestic, effortless flight. Surely the King of birds. But let's get things in their right perspective. Certain beasts and birds have only man to control their numbers. This is a fact of life that all too many townees overlook. We must get a balanced outlook on our countryside or else we'll be taken over by the conservation lobby.

I've always said to Sally that May is the month to visit Argyll, when one can forget the 80 odd inches of rain, the midges and the tourists and enjoy the glory of the Azaleas, the Rhododendrons, to hear one's first cuckoo and to see that wonderful first flush of spring. So we headed off last week with our sights set on the Ardkinglas Estate which I managed a quarter of a century ago. After I left the estate it was split in two for succession purposes, and I thought then that young Johnnie Noble had got the worst of the deal because he got the hardest of the hill ground, miles of shores of Loch Fyne and a very busy main road running beside his main steading.

How wrong I have proved to have been as he has turned the shore line into first class oyster and mussel beds and offshore he has let out a salmon farm. The steading next to the road had had a smoker installed and includes a shop and an oyster bar.

Johnnie did what so many Scottish Lairds have failed to do in the past, he procured the services of someone who really knew about the job in the shape of Andy Lane who had served a long and hard apprenticeship in fish farming. And what an excellent partnership they make. Oysters of course were like salmon in the old days, eaten by rich and poor alike. It is only scarcity value that put these two delectable fish into the Yuppie market but with units such as I saw at Clachan Loch Fyne they are coming back to be comparable with other take-away foods, and much tastier and healthier too.

In the old days in Edinburgh they had oyster 'howffs' where people ate oysters and washed them down with wine, but pollution in the Forth plus over-fishing put a stop to that. This is where the head of Loch Fyne is ideal as there is no pollution and the oysters are reared on metal racks that can be moved by tractor so that the properly sized oysters can be selected. As the oysters are used to being out of water when the tide is out and then 'clam up' (to use a phrase) they can be safely shipped overseas to Hong Kong, Belgium and France. So I was witnessing a real success story. The nice thing is that the sheep, the sporting interests and the Forestry are not being forgotten and the latter has improved dramatically since my day (probably because of my absence!) and grow cones can be seen everywhere.

Yes it was great to see diversification really working at Ardkinglas where 20 locals are employed. And with the tenants employing another 30 this is real progress in revitalising the Highlands.

After a tour of the Estate and the smokehouse I sat in the oyster bar, which had been converted from the old byre, and as I relished the oysters I thought on how 25 years ago I had been shovelling you-know-what in that same shed. But I decided it was better to 'tuck in' than 'muck out'.

I little thought back in the hungry 1930s when I was learning shepherding in Ettrick (for pocket money) and living on poached salmon and braxy mutton, that I was doing anything to help animal disease research in Scotland. We used to moan like hell because we had to fit in a lot of extra gatherings so that a most amusing and kindly 'boffin' called Dr. Russell Greig could take endless blood samples from the tick infested ewe stock. It was from his work that the Animal Disease Research Association produced the Loupin' Ill vaccine that was to do so much for Scottish Hill Flocks.

And if you had told me in those far off days that I was to be guest speaker at Moredum Research Institute in Edinburgh I would have told you to go 'and bile yer heid'. But so it was last week when Chairman, Jim Stobo, decided that with the imminent cut in research grants to the institute he should call his directors together and hold a seminar. The directors are made up of representatives from each farming county and the list reads like a livestock farmers' Debrett.

I think I was asked to speak because I once said on this programme that 'there were too many scientists and not enough grieves' and my reason for saying it was that I had just listened to a scientist talking, for all too long, and away above my head on the need for more pure science. Since then I have been a regular visitor to Moredum and a dedicated subscriber. It would only take £10 p.a. per head from 8,000 farmers to make a substantial difference to the institute's income and when one thinks of the difference Loupin' ill, white scour and more recently the sheep pneumonia vaccines have made to our industry it's not asking a lot. Those three are only a very small part of the splendid work. *End of commercial.*

It was strange that my original tie-up with Moredum should have been when I was in the Borders as in the same week I had decided to have a day off and see more of my Border pals at the Lauderdale Point-to-Point (that is those pals who weren't at the Langholm Sevens).

May

I have always said it is so cold at Mosshouses that I'm sure the 'Peewits' don't fly until they are two years old, but perhaps this year they may do a bit better as it was warmer.

On my way to the races I saw the worst field of winter barley that it has been my (questionable) pleasure to view. However two hill farmers whom I met later and knew the field assured me they had fields equally bad. How long are those in upland areas going to act like the Gadarine swine spending oodles of money on spray and fertilisers, when their hills were made for stock. But what a grand sight for a stockman to see those real Blue Grey cows belonging to Will Hogg and his son running on the hill next to the Mosshouses and looking real well. I'll bet my bottom dollar they're worth a deal more money than a bad crop of winter barley.

I had a wonderful hour with Will, now 86, reliving the halcyon days of the pedigree export bull trade when he was a director of British Livestock Exports and I was at Millhills. He was commiserating with me on our grass sickness losses and telling me that one year he was off to judge the Royal Show at Newcastle and went out to take a quick look at his beasts first. He had two super Clydesdale Geldings sold to go to the Edinburgh Cleansing Department and he noticed one had started grass sickness. By the time he got home they were both dead and within a week his daughter Sheila had lost her famous Pony Club pony. Aye, if you look around there's always someone worse off than yourself.

I had heard, as I'm sure most of you have, that Orkney was an island of farmers who owned a boat but Shetland was made up of fishermen who had a croft. Well I went off to see how true the second part of the saying was, as often though I'd been to Orkney I'd never been to Shetland.

For the whole week I was there the wind never shifted out of the North and as there is hardly a tree on the island winter woollies were the order of the day. I was sorry I'd taken my kilt and left my longjohns at home.

May

Cold it might have been but the warmth of the islanders was typical of so many in the remoter areas of this country. Unlike Orkney, there are few really fertile areas on the main island but Ally Flaws, whom I had met before, lived in one of them. He is the sort of farmer that is going to make a comfortable living no matter how tough the going, because firstly he, his wife and his son are all workers. Secondly he hasn't spent money on a lot of fancy cars, equipment or useless concrete (in fact he showed me round in an ageing car that he had difficulty in starting). And thirdly he is taking his produce right through to the customer as he has a thriving wee butcher's shop and he is in the middle of building a new shop on the Lerwick-Sunburgh airport road.

In the shop and the slaughter house he employs four men, all young and all good workers glad to have a job since the oil boom days are over. As an outsider looking in I would say that oil has been a mixed blessing to the island as it gave it roads, schools, leisure centres, etc but also a higher standard of living which is going to be hard to keep up. Also it had the worst planning I have ever seen, with crops of ghastly looking houses that have sprung up like mushrooms. Not everyone can, like Ally, butcher their own stock but at Dingwall, in Shetland, Miss Sandison from Stirlingshire has set up an excellent Agricultural Museum where I especially enjoyed seeing the Tuskers and floachter spades for cutting peat and these are still in use to this day. There were wee Shetland sheep everywhere and they seem to survive on nothing.

But fish is still king and as in farming the big boys have done tremendously well and stories abound of fishermen in rough jerseys signing vast cheques for BMWs! And as in farming the wee boys are having it tough. When one thinks that a lamb sent to the mainland has between £4 and £5 transport costs on it no wonder living prices are high but might I suggest that one way the small fisherman could make money is to keep his good local fish for visitors like myself in hotels - where I was offered nothing but fried haddock. I can do better in Perthshire!

I hate computers, and all electric gadgets bred the same way. My son, who makes his living from being an agricultural computer buff, says it's because I can't add two and two! But it's not because of my general uselessness

45

with electrical equipment, it's because computers do away with labour. We used to be famous in Scotland for our coal, our steel, our ships and our farming but now we seem to be turning into a country that is putting together electrical equipment of every different type and description.

When I complained to my son that computerising a farm was keeping the farmer's boot off the soil, which is still the only way to run a unit, he countered by saying that, on the contrary, a properly computerised farm should give the farmer *more* time to walk his farm.

Well I don't know, as an old friend of mine keeps saying, but what I do know is of a case of an Estate in the Highlands which was looking well, produced good stock, employed good labour and is now looking a mess, employs the barest of labour, and why? Because it's being run by a computer from the stockbroking belt! And I'm seeing farms where the farmer is arable orientated and is doing all his cropping work timeously but is neglecting his stock because the computer tells him that X acres should only employ Y men (or more likely none at all).

When the computers were first employed by the Auction Marts I was the first to howl in protest (not only because until they got used to them the staff were at sea and at the autumn sales there were endless delays) but much more because one lost that most valuable of all things, the *personal* touch, that wee gossip with the clerk about the weather, the prices and how good the stock were looking (or, if your neighbour's, how bad!).

When at pedigree sales in the South they started using videos of stock for sales I thought the end of the world had come. But I was wrong. The end of my world has come now as I hear a well known Scottish mart is organising a computerised sale for ordinary store stock. I suppose that means one sends the details of your beast - age, sex, breed or cross, weight, etc. But how does that replace the personal touch, the crack, the shopping spree and the fellowship that have always gone with market day.

Turn in your graves, me old pals with whom I have spent so many happy and instructive hours at Marts up and down the country. Things ain't what they used to be.

May

I have been known on this programme to have sworn about our Highland Ponies and the girls' event horses, but no way today. Sal and I are just home from a smashing, free, eight-day holiday thanks to our driving pony Rosy. Our breed show last year was sponsored by Brittany Ferries as their French Chairman breeds Highland ponies and we won one of the three prizes.

What changes I saw in their agriculture since last I was there some years ago. Our sponsors started with one ferry 15 years ago and now have five and another huge new one to be launched this summer. With the result that there has already, not waiting for 1992, been a tremendous two-way trade with this country.

Gone sadly are most of that lovely breed of cattle, the Normandie, to be replaced by Friesian/Holsteins imported from this country, although one farmer did tell me that he still made his delicious cheese from Normandie cow's milk. Sadly gone too are the Onion Johnnies whom many of you will remember complete with berets, their strings of onions strung over their bicycle handlebars, a common sight in Scotland 30 years ago. They have been replaced by a highly efficient vegetable co-operative who not only market this district's produce of onions, cauliflower, and artichokes but operate an up-to-date research station which has already produced some strains of earlier ripening varieties. Once again we are the prime market through the Ferry Ports. The use of plastic sheeting to warm the ground and keep down the weeds is widespread especially for the maize crop which is their main winter feed.

One thing hadn't changed, that was their reliance on electric fences as in a week's travelling I never saw a single animal - be it cow, sheep, goat or horse - that wasn't being kept in its field by an electric wire.

Talking of horses, there is about to be an explosion in the pony world over there as up to now a government quango has stated that any farm that comes on the market must by farmed and if it is not bought by a farmer then the quango will buy it. With the farming recession - and on small farms they are having it as well as us - the quango are left with so many properties that the rumour is they will soon rescind the rule. And then enter the yuppies followed by the ponies. I learn t all about this at a horse fair, where I thought that horses and ponies were already making far more than here. There were some hardy looking horse dealers who might well have been in Stirling,

Aberdeen, Perth or, for that matter, Ireland. Why is it all horse dealers look alike? Then there was a super demonstration of their native Breton Cart horses, look alikes to our Suffolk Punches, which are still used for vegetable cultivation because of their manoeuvrability in small fields. But the joke is that because of their narrow roads and distance from their homesteads you get the incongruous sight of a huge draught horse driven to his work in a tractor bogey!! Then there was a shoeing demonstration but as it takes two farriers to show a horse out there I don't think Brian, our blacksmith, would be that amused. Nor would I want to pay two bills.

The afternoon's entertainment would be the envy of any Scottish Show Committee - jousting Lippiezaners, horse quadrilles, a Houdini in chains, performing dogs, fire-eaters, country dancing etc, and all performed by the same eight people. Incredible. As for the available grub, which was from a series of barbecues, my mouth still waters at the thought of it!

Well! Have your sent off for your subsidy form for growing rice as an alternative crop to barley? Winter for the past eighteen months and no sign of improvement, so it's no joking matter but very serious for every farmer in the country. On one farm not a thousand miles from Woodburn, 200 acres of winter cereals have been ploughed in, and all crops, especially grass, are looking very jaundiced except the oil seed rape which isn't looking yellow enough, and far too many fields look patchy.

Another farmer of my acquaintance has had to put his cows and calves onto one of his hay fields because of the grass shortage. It's the sort of year that makes me think of one of my Dad's stories when he chided his session clerk, who was a farm grieve, for not attending church during a soaking wet harvest and the grieve pointed to heaven with this thumb and said 'Him and me's no speaking' and as I survey my garden where only two tatties, four broad beans and a solitary pea are all that has surfaced although in the ground for a month, I feel the same as that farm grieve.

But all has not been gloom and doom. That first class stockman Findlay McGowan has been on TV, full of enthusiasm for the future, and his reasons for that enthusiasm were his own proven good stockmanship. I'm always a wee bit sad that when the Luing Cattle-owners naturally bum about their breed of cattle they don't spare a thought for the first cross Highlanders which were the foundation of their breed and bred by my old boss and mentor, Duncan Stewart. They have the hybrid vigour that the Luing has lost.

There has been one sunny day in May when Sally was driving our novice Highland pony mare at Islabank and I was adjudicating one of the hazards. But even on that day I couldn't get away from farming as the Bank who looked after my overdraft for years had me in for a 'refresh'. Their manager asked me what I thought about the future of the industry as he was worried stiff about some of the farming overdrafts he was carrying. I told him quite frankly that he and his like were more that partly responsible for the plight of some farmers who have had money thrown at them, also to blame was the government that pushed us all into producing more and that gave capital grants for which many farmers had to borrow to make up the other 50 per cent.

I was telling a friend of mine (who is head of one of the country's best known Estate Agents) of my conversation with the Banker. He replied 'We've just taken over an Estate which has to find £135,000 per annum to service its overdraft'. I wished him the best of British luck but methinks he'll have some sleepless nights.

I've just heard an Aberdeenshire dairy farmer on the radio say that those on arable land had no alternative to cropping but the hill men could change to salmon fishing, grouse shooting, deer stalking, tourism etc. What a lot of poppycock! How little he knows the Highlands, even less the Uplands which have no sporting facilities and need every halfpenny to survive, never mind make a profit.

If, as the said gentleman asserts, the arable farmers have no alternative why have I seen in my time the switch from oats to spring barley, then winter barley, then peas, then oil seed rape back to winter wheat (because it happened to be paying well). And then there are always turnips, swedes or rape on which they can fatten the hill man's lambs and cast ewes and double their money on them for a few months' keep, although the hill man has had the keep of the ewe and all the lambing problems etc.

And what about the dairy farmer, who must have seen the surplus situation a mile off? He can take his calves right through and sell them as so-called beef animals.

But back to the hill and Upland farmer. He has only two crops, sheep and cattle, and he is desperately dependent on the Good Lord, as we all are in farming, because bad winters and springs can cost him a bomb. The hills of Scotland have always been, and I hope always will be, the reservoir of stock and men to the arable lands. As for turning those stockmen into keepers and stalkers or Bed and Breakfasters, the proud stockmen I have known have always had a friendly rivalry with the aforesaid.

I've managed the Moor of Rannoch for a quarter of a century so I ask, how do you get more deer or grouse on to miles and miles of damn-all, and a quango doesn't help by making it into a S S I. This, I might say, means Site of Special Interest, so I am not allowed to kill the hoodie crows, foxes etc which do so much damage.

Talking of quangos I hear that two high ranking M L C chiefs who wanted to see the bull testing station at Kinermony came North by plane to Dalcross, took a taxi to Kinermony, after a night in the most expensive hotel, took a taxi back, spent another night in the hotel and then took the plane South. Meantime two Scottish members who didn't manage to catch up with their Southern counterparts went to London and spent a night in a hotel. I can't see that exercise costing less that £2,000 of *our* money. We never asked for the M L C, it was foisted on us! I have a lot of time for their fieldsmen but they have always been top heavy with non practical boffins who cost us far too much.

The west coasters have that lovely saying 'that when the Lord made time he made plenty of it' and it is for that reason that I take myself off to Mull for a few days each May. I have never seen things so far behind as they were this year. Usually the grass on the island is weeks ahead of us in Strathearn, but not this year, and even the usually balmy south west wind seemed to be blowing cold. Nor did I get my favourite view in the world, that from Calgary Castle out over its silver sands and past its towering cliffs to the rollers of the Atlantic - for there was torrential, horizontal rain.

May

All the way from Crieff to Dervaig I passed lean hill ewes. I think in the past fifty years I've never seen hill ewes so thin, this when nowadays every hill farmer worth his salt feeds his sheep - not like the old days when it was a case of 'the survival of the fittest'.

There are some horrific stories of death among sheep and shortage of milk and I heard of one slaughter-man, who collects carcasses, telling a friend of mine that it would be a week before he could collect his fallen stock so great was his waiting list.

Nobody likes talking of his own bad lambing percentages but lambings of as low as 50 percent and lower are being bandied about on the north facing places. That where the white grass caught the East winds of the early spring and where there is no heather or draw moss - those two saviours on any good hill farm.

But bad though the weather may have been in the west they were spared that awful night of snow that swept the Borders and other east coast hills. One man of my acquaintance lost 130 lambs that night and another some 30. Thank God for the resilience of our hill farmers and their shepherds as they have a lot to contend with.

But at least on Mull they don't have foxes, which are reaching frightening proportions especially near forestry plantations where the trees are growing up and the vole population is decreasing as a result, leaving the foxes with little alternative but lambs for food. In a recent letter to the Scottish Farming News the writer said he was one of the large number in this country who had believed foxes didn't kill lambs - until he started losing them himself and then he shot an old dog fox and the killing ceased. I remember well when I factored the Ben Challum Estate we had a neighbour, one Wattie Burton of Cononish, who was red hot on foxes and knew exactly where the vixen would be if the killings were in a certain area. As if it was yesterday, I can see him pushing his hand over his nose and saying 'she'll be in the Tol Dhu' and sure enough she was.

Mull was so relaxing and so sleep making (I did 10-12 hours nay bother) that I feel a new man. And talking of men I was told 'the men from the Monastry' were coming to visit the farm on which I was staying and I expected to see some Abbots, Monks or Friars to walk in, only to meet some old friends from the Department of Agriculture still known in these far flung places as the Ministry of Agriculture. So hence the 'Men from the Monastry'.

June

Horses have played a very big part in my life. My first job was with them and it looks as if I'm destined to end my days as a groom just as I began them. When we were up at the farm and the girls, including Sal, had ponies that were continually needing mucking out, eating nothing but the best of hay, chasing the lambs, nibbling the top of my newly planted beech hedge, breaking out on the main road at night and having to be recaught by torchlight or worst of all dying of grass sickness (and we had nine in 22 years) I used to call them 'osses bloody osses', And recently it has been nothing but 'osses bloody osses'. First it was the horse driving trials at Islabank where I was officiating. This is a fast growing sport as are all horse events. What has this to do with farming? Well, just everything as horses have to be bred and fed and most of both are directly connected with farming. The Royals' interest in all equestrian events has had a lot to do with the sport's growing popularity Prince Philip was competing at Islabank and I'm only sad that he drives Fells and not Highland ponies as the latter are making a great comeback since the days when they were the only means of carrying grouse and deer off the hill, now largely done by mechanical transport such as snowcats, agrocats etc.

Since a Highland Pony mare won the coveted supreme ridden award for Mountain & Moorland Ponies at Olympia, the demand has shot up with the result that many farmers who bred Highland Ponies and got a colt foal and didn't want the cost of having it castrated, and just sold it as a colt, will be thinking twice as the present demand is for broken geldings.

Then it was on to see the New Gleneagles Hotel Equestrian Centre being opened by the Princess Royal where anyone with any Scots blood in their veins would be proud to see the parade of Scottish horses, Lucius, Rubstic, Flying Ace, Ian Stark on Sir Wattie (after their historic win at Badminton) to name but a few. One local farmer has decided to turn his farm over to horses as the demand for stabling and fodder for the planned events at Gleneagles will be immense.

Then to round off the horsey fortnight Sal and I were judging them at the Gargunnock Show; one of those super small confined shows set in the most wonderful scenery. It was a real pleasure to give the Championship to a wee lass riding a super child's pony; the look of joy on her face when she got the rosette was more than recompense for giving up a day in the garden. I always say that wee girls have three loves in life, teddy bears, 'osses and boyfriends

53

in that order. Thank God mine are now on the third as they cost less to keep than 'bloody 'osses'.

Roll on next week and I can get back to my usual routine of:- the Nine O'clock News, Weather Forecast, run the dogs, shut up the hens, check the horse in the stable, tap the barometer then bed and a good book. My idea of bliss has been shattered these past four weeks.

My involvement with our 1987 Election has been minimal but I did enjoy attending a political meeting in Mull where, during the proceedings, in staggered a gently fu' shepherd complete with dog which had a great time running round and round the hall and of course had to cock its leg at one of the chairs. Thank God for the West and their complete disregard for time and for what is looked on as normal practice in the rest of the country. Not only did this meeting have its drunk shepherd plus dog, it was held a day later than scheduled. That to my mind is putting Politics in proper prospective.

What an eyeopener I had when I went out West this year, their lambs are looking terrific, really sappy and lots of twins and not one bauchly lamb did I see, a complete change to last year. I just hope that the exporters have things lined up for the Autumn sales: by what I've seen there will be more than enough for the home market.

I was in Mull to look at some Highland cattle that are now, like the Galloways, in great demand overseas. On the way over on the boat I was reading in the Scottish Farmer how entries in the Blackfaces at shows fluctuated depending on who was judging. Nothing new in this, but the SF suggested the Blackfaces could be divided in two as were the Cheviots with their North/ South divide. I was thinking about stock divisions when I passed the Calgary Estate in Mull which was namely when I was a boy for what we called the Western Isles type of Highland Pony whereas the Mainland ponies had more bone and were referred to as Garrons, the former being favoured for riding and the later for croft work or pannier and deer ponies. There will always be variations on a theme, as my musical friends would call differences within a breed, and long may it continue in our striving for excellence.

June

Ian Morrison has been speaking about his image of the tweed-jacketed grouse-shooting lairds and how that was changing in his view. My dear Ian, as in every walk in life there have always been different sorts in the landed gentry class. Highland Estates especially have depended on money from other sources to prime the pump so to speak. In my time I have seen Glasgow ship-building money, Bristol tobacco money, London banking money etc. In fact in the Highlands they said 'where there's a will they're away'. All kinds of money has been pumped into the rural economy, and a dashed good thing too. Now we have German, Dutch and French money flooding in as Europeans realise what a lovely countryside we have and how good our sport can be. A constant change of ownership from all sources, but it was ever thus.

But through all this change there has run a seam of Scottish Lairds who have lived on their Estates and run them from home. Among the bigger ones the Buccleuchs and Douglas Homes in the Borders and the Lochiels and Lovats in the Highlands and many more besides. But the interesting change to me is how the younger modern lairds are training themselves to run their family Estates. One of the curses of the pre-war and just-post-war days was that the laird's son went to an English Public school then possibly Oxbridge and in later days Cirencester; came home with a pair of cricket pads, green wellie boots and a yearning to go back South to the flesh pots, but had lost the touch to manage his men, with perhaps the exception of the head keeper or stalker. But this is changing rapidly and I think one of the reasons is the ease of transport to Australia and New Zealand. Why? because in my young day it took weeks not hours to get there, and if a young man went out there he usually stayed out there, whereas now he goes out, learns to work with stock, and be one of Jock Tamson's bairns - for there is no doffing of bonnets out there - and he'll probably wonder if he has a father or mother as their term of endearment questions one's parentage.

I had reason to meet one of these modern lairds last week when I went to see his mother's Highland ponies, one of the few studs left that are genuinely reared on hill ground, consequently slower to mature, but as a result famed for their longevity. This young laird knew his sheep, was building a new shed along with his two men, was telling a fencer where he wanted the fence to go and during the hour I was in the house was booking in someone for the salmon fishing and arranging for their Australian help to go to a local ceilidh by talking on christian name terms to the organiser. In fact a laird who knew his job and was acceptable in the district. What a change, and for the better. And most important of all are the modern lairds' wives, no longer house proud but lambers, calvers, ghillies, cooks, mothers and general supporters. Although only a laird of few acres, I've got one too. God bless her!

What do you do with yourself now that you're retired Ben? If I've been asked that question once I've been asked it a dozen times. Well, this Thursday I judge the stirks at the Highland Show, jump on a plane for London and get to Chelmsford to judge the Murray Greys on Friday morning, go to Cambridge that afternoon to see daughter Philippa, return to Chelmsford to judge the Highland ponies on Saturday morning and the Mountain & Moorland championship in the afternoon. Back that night on the train for Kirk and to open the ever-increasing mail I get, as a District Councillor, and try to digest the oodles and oodles of reports it contains. Off on Monday at 6.00 am for the Royal Highland to show a Highland pony of our breeding that we sold to a friend. Then on Tuesday I sit in the licensing court (who better?) and as the person in charge of Industry in Perth & Kinross meet the directors of a well known blend of whisky to hear them spell out their future plans, then in the evening the Perth Theatre executive meeting followed by its AGM and a farewell supper to the retiring Chairman and on Wednesday our monthly Council meeting. Never mind, the rest of the week's my own.

As you can imagine, in two counties such as Perth and Kinross we are extremely exercised about the future of the farming industry. Up until now planning permission in the countryside has just not been allowed because quite frankly some of the buildings were so out of keeping with their surroundings that they were a blot on the landscape. Also the Department of Agriculture used to put the foot down if the land to be built on was first class arable land. But things have changed dramatically now as we are over produced. Don't let's fool ourselves, land is going to be taken out of production, and sooner than many people think. I don't want to see thousands of hectares of weeds blowing all over our green and pleasant land. I thought Maitland Mackie's idea, propounded at a discussion in Belfast, that planning authorities should allow ten acre plots to be sold for housing around our cities with planning permission for only one dwelling house is not the stupidest of ideas: (a) people buying these plots would be determined to look after them and there are still plenty of folk not two generations away from farming with a strong urge to own land and get their hands dirty with soil, and (b) it would take, he reckoned, a million acres of land out of production.

Why I like this tentative idea is that it would leave the bread basket of Britain, ie the eastern counties virtually untouched and the hills and uplands (with all subsidies given to them if I had my way) producing the stock. For me in my small way as part of a planning authority I'm for more houses in the countryside but they must be tasteful, not just wooden boxes.

As to next week and the Royal Highland a big brown envelope marked RHAS arrived at Woodburn in March and I said to Sal 'Whoopee having judged the Highland cattle and ponies they are asking me obviously to do one of the interbreed Championships'. On opening the letter it contained an invitation to judge the crooks and walking sticks, which I was thrilled to accept. The committee have obviously never seen one of my attempts at home carving but it was good for my conceit.

June

Although I love my native land dearly I always enjoy my forays over the Border. My last was to judge the Highland cattle at the Three Counties Show in Malvern. A dashed good turn out they were and a credit to the breed, The only thing I don't enjoy is driving on motorways so we left at 5.00 am and got off the motorway in Gloucestershire at lunch time, and was I ready to enjoy a pint at one of England's greatest attractions, a village pub! As I sat sipping my pint, in the pub garden, and it was Sunday lunchtime and therefore busy, I couldn't help noticing that of the ten pairs of shoes worn by those around me I was the only one who wore leather: all the rest were plastic, canvas or other ersatz materials.

Yet I understand the tannery business is flourishing and when I chipped a friend of mine about the high price of sheep at one period last year he said the skins were worth a bomb so is leather becoming too dear or are our beasts' hides not what they were, or have we become a throw-away nation who wants our shoes only for a few months. I certainly haven't helped the leather trade much as my kilt brogues were made for me in Perth 42 years ago.

But at the same time that I was taking stock of the shoes I noticed that all the ladies and many of the men had wool pullovers - although it was sunny there was a breeze blowing. If one multiplies the people in that pub by the people who wear woollen garments in this Country why oh why is wool cheap and hides dear. For wool is the one farming commodity that hasn't risen appreciably in my time. Oh! I know someone will say that Blackfaced wool with which I'm most acquainted is used for Italian mattresses and carpets but especially the latter have gone through the roof since I set up house. Gone are the days when one's wool clip used to pay for the ewes' winter feed (the small amount they got 30 years ago) and pay for wintering the hoggs. Nowadays it would pay one more to breed hill sheep that bore no fleeces like Dorset Horns (though God help them in a good going Highland blizzard), than go through the expense and hassle of the days needed for the clipping. At least in the old days we all neighboured with each other ,and one could hear oneself speak, the gossip and crack was good (and the drams were immense!) but now it's all contractors with their noisy electric machines throwing off astronomic amounts of fleeces in a day.

And when it comes to wintering hoggs why didn't the diversification scheme allow for grassland on farms to be allowed to be set aside for the specific purpose of wintering hill hoggs which would help arable and hill farmers alike. I fear me the days have gone when I used to argue with Speyside farmers whether the wintering per head was to be 5/- or 5/3d (25 or 26.5p new money) but thank God the conditions under which those Speyside farmers used to live have also gone.

I wasn't at the Highland Show on Sunday, because I'm agin Sunday events as I feel we all need one day a week to recharge the batteries, if not at church then just resting, but my goodness what a success story the Highland Show opening has been, and wrong I have been proved. Who ever thought of a 55,000 paid entry on Sunday, a quite magnificent achievement. They tell me the mix of the main ring events was just right for the townies, and don't let's fool ourselves, *they* are the people we want to pull in. The only way we are going to halt our present bad public image, always greatly distorted, is to let the people in the towns see how we operate and why.

Another way that publicity has helped farmers has been popularity of the sheep dog demonstrations, thanks to TV's 'One Man and his Dog'. Being a hopeless handler myself but as one who has up to last month always had a collie, I am full of admiration for these men. I always remember the late Jim Wilson, to me the Prince of handlers, being given some fearfully wild sheep at a Royal Show demonstration in front of the Queen Mum. One sheep - they were big three year old wethers - dashed up the steps beside the Royal Box and stood there. Jim, as cool as a cucumber, sent the great Nap up through the crowds and when the wether faced up to him, stamping his feet, Jim shouted 'Tak a haud'. Nap, who was known to have a bit of a grip in him, did just that in the wether's nose. End of story.

Being a reluctant arable farmer I had never visited the plots so beautifully laid out on the West side of the showground but as my eldest son is now quite high up in the firm that plants them I thought I must remedy my years of omission. No wonder we have surplus food when one sees the fantastic strides we have made in seed varieties, fertilisers, and management.

I know it's a sure sign of old age but it seems but yesterday that one talked of two ton an acre wheat crops with bated breath. Now if you're not in the four-ton league you're 'oot the windae'. The new hill grass mixtures especially intrigued me, I think there's a great future there. What a crying shame this research and our efficiency have led to good food we can't use and - because of world politics - others can't have.

I enjoyed judging the crooks and sticks at the Highland but was sad that there were not more entries. Could it have been because of the person who was judging? Or could it be that certain names have dominated this section, making newcomers wary of entering? I don't know but of one thing I'm certain: since I judged this section some ten years ago the winners were of the same high standard but the overall show has improved dramatically.

I have been to the Essex County Show to judge the overall Beef Championship.

What is it about us farmers that there is nothing we enjoy more than farming other people's places and gloating over them if they are making a middling job? So from London to Chelmsford I enjoyed every second in the train doing just that. It's mostly heavy land and as a result their winter wheat was looking extra good but after that awful spring their spring crops were much as other areas up and down the country. Being a predominantly arable county the stock that I saw, with the exception of the Friesians, were bad to say the least. When one sees what passes for beef cattle in the South of England one wonders how anyone down there eats beef.

Next day doing the inter-breed championship I had an exceptionally good Simmental cow in front of me; with a top like a billiard table and set on four really good legs and needless to say brought out by a Scot. But overall the standard of beef cattle was nothing like as high as the Friesians and although I am no Scottish Nationalist there is no doubt at all that the huge Scottish influx to Essex in the past half century, many bringing their Ayrshires with them, had a great influence on the stockmanship of the Southern Counties. I found this when I went to Sussex in the 1930s where my boss the head cattleman used to leave stale feeds in front of his so called show cattle and wondered why when he topped up the trough the beasts wouldn't eat it.

Forgetting the stock side, the big difference between the English Shows and our Highland is in the standard of stands selling produce, knitwear, shoes

June

etc. Having time on my hands in Essex I toured these as I did in the Exhibition hall at the Highland, and the difference was chalk and cheese. I never did like the Exhibition Hall but this year with but a few exceptions the contents were a disgrace to our country.

When the Spaniard asked the Mulach, a man from Mull, what the Gaelic equivalent was for the word 'Manyana' the reply was that there was no such word with the same sense of urgency. I don't know if it is because the Mulachs firmly believe that when the Lord made time he made plenty of it that first made me fall in love with the Island and its people but for forty years I have been visiting it. Back in the 1930s my late father and Archie Craig, later to be one of our best Church of Scotland Moderators, were to be the first two to back George MacLeod, now Lord MacLeod of Fuinary in his project of getting unemployed from Govan to help in the rebuilding of the Abbey in Iona. And in my schoolboy days I used to love to hear Dad talk about Mull and Iona. But it was after the last war that I got to know it well when I was asked to do the odd advisory job for people with no agricultural background who seemed to be attracted to Mull like bees to oil seed rape. The saying was that just post war the Island was full of 'Mad Majors and Dotty Doctors' and it was one of the latter who asked me to advise him on his Estate at Glengorm (without much success I might say as he was too kind and wouldn't get rid of some charming but idle men). I well remember going over on the old Lochinvar with that gentleman of a skipper the late Calum Black. It was blowing a gale and Calum wasn't sure whether to sail or not but said to the Doctor that he would send word to us in what was then the Station Hotel if he was going. As the time went on and there was no summons the Doctor and I got down to a bit of serious drinking and after at least an hour old Alec the Boots burst in to say that Calum had been blowing his hooter for a least quarter of an hour! The Lochinvar could easily roll to a 45 degree angle but the Doctor and I, the only passengers, were completely oblivious to the storm and thoroughly enjoyed our crack with the gallant captain!

But all that has changed and with the advent of the roll-on roll-off ferries no longer do the farmers have to man handle two hundred weight wire-tied bales of Timothy Hay on and off the Lochinvar: the fodder now goes to their door on a lorry. So popular has the Island become that this summer most of the ferries, and they ply back and forth every second hour, are already fully booked. Even a fortnight ago when I was taking a Highland Pony over I had to book, and on the way home six cars were left waiting for the next ferry.

Naturally the success story has affected the farming scene as well, Although far too much of the Island has been afforested, the land improvement with reseeding, liming, slagging and fencing grants has transformed the stock and their own little slaughterhouse has given the numerous hotels and Bed & Breakfast farms and houses really good local meat. Now they have a first class bakery in Tobermory so no longer will that ghastly white sliced stodgy plastic packed bread, the bane of the Western Isles, be the main cargo on the ferries.

But not all the farmers on the Island have gone in for big expensive schemes and the person to whom I delivered my pony, my old friend Archie McCuish, is a believer in a low-input low-output system. Archie served in the war and when he came out was shepherding in Glenlochay when I managed that Estate and after other shepherding jobs - and in the 1950s and

1960s shepherds moved much more than they do now - he got the tenancy from the Department of Agriculture and then the chance to buy his farm in Mull. He relied heavily on the seaweed for his ewes' winter feed, and some neighbours feel that he would do more with his subsidies but I have always maintained the hill subsidies should be social ones to keep people there.

The next week I was in Aberdeenshire on District Council business and between Inverurie, Kintore and Aberdeen I saw some middling crops of spring barley, probably sown at the wrong time and leeched as a result, but when I thought of some of those arable farmers' ageing combines and mounting overdrafts and the future of cereals, I decided I'd plump for the McCuish System.

July

I have now been to five summer shows either judging, showing or commentating.

I love 'em dearly except for one thing, those boring cold lunches with the overdone stringy roast beef, the lettuce leaf that looks and tastes as if it was left over from last year's show and the interminable cold chicken that tastes of nothing at all. Broadcaster Tom Graham summed it up when talking of the 15-year inflation, foreign cars up 40 per cent, beef a mere ten per cent and chicken the same as fifteen years before and just as tasteless!

But I've had one good cold lunch this summer and that was at Moredun when the ADRA had their AGM and we were told by Lord Gray of Contin (Hamish to some of us) that the Priorities Board had recommended a significant decrease in public funding of animal disease work.

This is where we could all come in with a bit of self help. For less than the price of a bottle per annum we could help the magnificent research work Moredun does. I'll bet every livestock producer has at some time used a vaccine or serum produced by a commercial company but researched at Moredun.

But back to the lunch. It is not for nothing that Australians and New Zealanders use mutton rather than beef to feed their shearers and stockmen. We had some lovely cold mutton at Moredun. It's a funny thing but many, of whom I am one, never tire of cold mutton as they do with other cold meats. What a perfect pest this radiation scare has been, as if we didn't have enough problems selling red meat without this scare. The great British public are 'Kittle Cattle' and can so easily be put off buying anything, but take a long time to be wooed back.

So full marks to those who arranged to have Scotch lamb for the famous wedding breakfast. This should go far to restore confidence in eating lamb although as yet we don't know from where the lamb is to come. It can scarcely be from Braes of Balquhidder lambs: they will need another month, I would guess. I hope the Royal couple get the lovely weather we have had in Strathearn where some super hay has been made and the tattie fields are looking exceptionally good and the roguers are out in force. I often wondered forty years ago when I managed for Sir Jas. Roberts why the tattie roguers always came at lunch time, then I saw their official forms (inadvertently left on the table while they went to the loo) with headlines saying 'Jolly good grub here'.

Not for the first time on this programme I quote my mother, now a sprightly 99 years old, who when things are going badly says 'The Lord moved in a mysterious way his *blunders* to perform' and so say I having come back from a sun-drenched Royal Show and a Yorkshire Show, where farmers were crying out for rain, and yet when I got back to Strathearn there were literally hundreds of acres of hay laying and getting yellower and yellower, and they are there still. It must be a long time since we had as cold and as wet a summer as this one and yet when I was in Wales, between judging the Highland Ponies at the Royal and the Yorkshire where I judged the Highland Cattle, my friend with whom I was staying was merrily baling the most lovely green hay just like the stuff we baled last year.

It's a pity the Royal has become so big that one can't get right round it in a day but at least the rolled umbrella, bowler hatted image is not so prevalent as it was, say, fifteen years ago - when I remember having a flaming row with a steward because on the Thursday he was allowing his horses to dung on the approach to the Aberdeen-Angus stand and as we weren't growing rhubarb (that year) I wasn't exactly chuffed!

But now all the horses are shepherded down horse lanes directly into their judging rings, a tremendous improvement. It was just great to be able to take advantage of the Aberdeen-Angus stand, in which I had so much say when it was erected. The in-hand Mountain and Moorland Championship was judged in the ring opposite the stand and I was able to make use of the large umbrellas and watch my Highland Pony Champion perform. He was a beautiful moving Gelding bred in Ayrshire by Mr. Hendrie and I was thrilled when he came reserve champion to the excellent Dartmoor. When I made him champion in the morning one of the leaders of one of the stallions was stupid enough to say to me that she had never seen a gelding triumph over a stallion before to which I replied 'Madam, if I owned a stallion with looks like your beast I'd have him cut and even then he wouldn't beat today's champion!'

At the Royal I had the chance to watch the Burke Trophy being judged and having had that honour four years ago my commiserations were with Robert Needham as he went through the final motions before giving the Trophy to an outstanding pair of Simmentals. All judging is a nerve wracking experience, as is broadcasting or public speaking, and if anyone says 'it's all too easy' and they don't get butterflies as far as I'm concerned they're not worth a damn. But somehow the Burke has an atmosphere all of its own with a superb run up by that ace commentator Raymond Brooks-Ward, and an international audience including international judges and very critical home judges rooting for their own breed. And remember the Trophy is for the best matched pair, one male and one female, of fifteen beef breeds. The year I judged there was an outstanding pair of Longhorns, a breed just about to go into the Rare Breeds Survival Trust. They were beautifully matched and oh boy, could they walk, something many of our latest imported breeds just can't do.

Well, I had the courage of my convictions and I put them up. Many of the country's real stockmen applauded me but the Monarch who was visiting the show last year was not amused. I was reminded of this on the Tuesday before I went South to the Show when Her Majesty was visiting the Caithness Glass Factory which is in my 'patch' as a District Councillor. The Lord Lieutenant introduced me as the local councillor to which Her Majesty replied 'He is more that that. He once gave the Burke Trophy to a pair of cattle, the only ones my carriage horses ever shied at'. How to be put in one's place by the No 1 in the land.

Not many, if any, of my listeners will have stood in a food queue because either you're too young to remember the time of queues or you were on a farm where rationing was virtually unknown. Being in the Forces, or hospital, I didn't have to queue either except on one occasion when I was staying in London with my surgeon, the great Sir Archie McIndoe, who stuck on my nose for me. He sent me out to queue for fish which was in extremely short supply. I thought the people queuing didn't look as if they could afford this expensive luxury and after a time I turned to the wizened old hag beside me and said 'This is the fish queue isn't it?' and she replied 'No it's spirits my dear.' In fact it was Meths.

I tell this story today because if certain things that we've been hearing about

this last week come about we will see food queues again in this country, maybe not in my time but in the next fifty years. Firstly the green house effect is definitely with us judging by the abnormal weather most parts of the world are being subjected to. The huge grain mountain, (which urban politicians and the urban populace have used as a big stick to beat our backs) is a myth and is no longer there. Then there's the organic lobby who see 20 per cent of our productive land being organic by the year 2000. That should produce lovely grub but it will be very expensive and low yielding as I found to my cost when I grew a field of oats with no nitrogen all those 25 years ago. Add set-aside to the foregoing, especially of our better land, and the result, given a drought or two, equals a bread queue in my book. Then the urban populace would realise what a first class job our industry has done since the war.

There has been talk of the possibility of grass fields being set aside but it would seem that few farmers look on their grass as a crop. No longer do they harrow and roll it in the spring (or if they do the latter the roller is driven so fast it bumps up and down and does little good). And how few fields one sees being topped to let the grasses come again from the roots. I had a boss once who planted a yard breadth of herbs in each grazing field which was always rumped bare. He reckoned that because of their long roots they brought up added minerals. But don't be like the yuppie farmer who saw his cows eating some scythed dead nettles so he decided to sow a field of them the next year - with painful results!

I'm a great believer that when one gives up a job one should get right out and not hassle the new incumbent. Hence I didn't go near the Blackmount Estate from the November when I retired until a fortnight ago. The day coincided with the 76th birthday of a mentor of mine, Fisher Ferguson who managed Glenartey, so along with another ex-keeper Baldie McNaughton, now in his 80s, we set off from St. Fillans through country we all knew.

It was a case of Memory Hold the Door, as each of us regaled the others with memories of places we passed. When it was Ben Vorlich, Fisher told us of the time he was told to run and cut off some hinds and when he got there he shot the first fourteen with as many shots and on returning home it turned out he had run five miles. Then it was Baldie's turn and he recalled how he had packed fifty-two wool bags in one day only to be told at the finish that as it was a grand moonlight night he would enjoy the walk home to St. Fillans, a mere six miles. They bred them tough in those days, and there they were still going strong.

Last week was the Smithfield Councils' quarterly meeting and it was held in the Food Research Institute at Bristol. Having spent an afternoon there, I and most of the council, who constitute some of the best known stockfarmers in Britain, couldn't make out what the Institute was trying to do. There were 120 scientists with all their own little empires costing a fortune and after a beef-tasting session (in a most plush room very expensively set up for the job) one scientist was not amused when 27 out of 30 of us preferred some steer meat rather than the bull beef. He said we were going against the normal trend. Well who the hell sets the trend, I asked 'You scientists I suppose who never owned a beast in your life'. Then another test they had was on the effect of hormones. As it looks as if these are to be scrapped next year that will be more money down the plug 'ole! If I was the Minister of Agriculture I'd scrap the whole thing and pour the millions saved into worthwhile projects like Craibstone or Moredun.

When I got home I thought how right my two old friends had been when they said 'Some people in agriculture don't know they're alive today compared with our young days'.

———————————

Because of my occasional appearances in the pulpit as a lay preacher, some of my clever friends call me Dr. Jekyll and Mr. Hyde. It was never more true than last weekend. On the Saturday in the morning, I did my stint at telling people where to park their lorries and floats (and believe me I would dearly have loved to tell one or two exactly where to go) and in the afternoon I had four hours doing the commentary. Nothing could have been more different. From the hustle and bustle of calling for and commentating on the different events, with the quiet (and sometimes not so quiet) oaths as stock attendants and stewards wilted gently in the glorious sunshine; to the two services I conducted on the Sunday where the boot was on the other foot. Dressed in my winter heavy black kilt jacket (handy for Highland weddings and funerals), I melted, not wilted, in the heat of this glorious spell. Oh! I know some of you will still be crying out for rain but as I said in one of my prayers, What do we know about droughts when you think of East Africa, or of floods when you think of India or Pakistan. As for volcanoes and hurricanes, they just belong to other countries.

I well remember a sermon delivered back in the 1930s by my old Dad (and I must admit I can't recall the details of many) when he said it was a good thing farmers didn't have the making of the weather as one would want rain for the neeps and another would want sunshine for the hay or the Highland Show, which was in his charge of Melrose that year.

And here we are fifty years on in the same boat. I for the first time have irrigated my vegetable garden and although I was eating my Duke of York tatties three weeks earlier than usual they are now far too big to have that lovely flavour that freshly dug small new spuds have. And when I see the amount of tattie crops being irrigated in this county I just wonder how much good it is doing for the consumer. Oh! I know it's giving a bigger crop to the producer but is it a better one and does it store as well?

As for the burns, streams and rivers that are being dried out by the irrigators, I can't see the green section of the community standing for that much longer. Grain yields are bound to be down especially on some of the poorer upland places that never should have grown white crops in the first place. But land that has been well handled will still yield well and if this weather continues the price will be up and the drying costs will be nil.

For me I'd rather be having my midday meal outside every day than donning oilskins and leggings to turn stooks whose heads were growing together - as I had to do all too often in the days of yore.

'What have they done to your favourite breed of cattle Ben?' This was the greeting I got from my local butcher the other day. And he wasn't talking about my beloved Highlanders but about the Aberdeen-Angus. In the same vein also a well known feeder of black cattle was looking at the parade of blacks at Braco Show and said that the majority weren't his type.

These two conversations came to me as I watched the parade of Blacks at the Black Isle Show and they were also under the scrutiny of their knowledgeable and popular patron the Queen Mum. I don't know what she thought of the show of her favourite breed but they were not for me! Long faces, sharp shoulders, bad tail heads, sickle hocks but worst of all split up the backside and with none of the rear end that made the breed famous. Oh! I know breeders listening to this will say it's a case of sour grapes, because I never bred a high priced bull as all the high priced ones in recent years have been tall standing with lots of air below them.

But it's a strange thing that both my friends the butcher and the feeder, both at the top of their trades, should be feeling a sense of disquiet too.

I do hope the breed gets its act together and doesn't continue to take on the so-called continentals in the 'size at all cost' stakes.

But if I thought the Aberdeen-Angus a middling lot the Highland Ponies that I was asked to judge at the Black Isle were a joy to see, all 120 of them! I was particularly chuffed that my champion mare with foal at foot went on to beat the Shetland, the Welsh and the in-hand Hunter pony and to finish up as overall pony champion and receiving a special sash commemorating this special 150th show, from none other than the Queen Mum herself.

The Black Isle have a special class for Highland Ponies in working tack, some with deer saddles, others grouse panniers, and then one dragging a log, while another had cart harness and there were 20 in the class. I luckily had a well known head stalker to judge the intricacies of local deer saddles etc and he was adamant that two ponies that I fancied should not be considered because they had no bits in their mouths, only head collars. Well, well, doctors differ!

After this magnificent show of ponies it was indeed a come down on the 'glorious' 12th (and it was glorious) to be taken up the hill in a modern agrocat, but I was mighty glad of the hurl, and after seven hours rough walking - and 22.5 brace of grouse in the bag - my legs told me I was 3 score years and ten.

It seems like yesterday - a great saying of the aged - when I took over the factorship of a well-known Inverness-shire sporting estate which also sported a fierce head stalker. As an opening gambit I said 'Any trouble with vermin Douggie?' and back came the reply 'Aye a puckle hoodies and a Factor'.

Well if the late Douggie was in this strath today he'd do his nut if he saw the rabbits and crows. I don't know if some farmers think it's a cure for our grain surpluses but one farm has a swathe of 30 yards wide absolutely ruined by rabbits and another has well over 200 rooks bashing down the barley morning and night. Then of course we have the other sort of farmers who are determined to get the last pea of grain (and rightly so as things are today) and round us we have not one but three bangers going night and day and at two in the morning I don't think they scare much vermin, except your s truly.

The show weather has so far been mixed. But we at Braco had a super day whereas Perth wasn't so lucky and as Braco is usually wet and Perth fine I doot the good Lord got his show calendar dates mixed up. But Arran seems to have had a super 150th show as I was delighted to hear from Archie McDiarmid, now 80, broadcasting like a veteran broadcaster. It was Archie who introduced me to showing back in the mid 1920s. Those were the days of horse transport, and hay-making was a happy occasion as well as a family one. I have a photo of twenty of us sitting round a hay cone taking our tea which always included home-baked scones and pancakes with honey and the day always ended with a dook in the 'pot' in the Machrie Burn.

It was on Machrie Farm that Archie shepherded so conscientiously for 38 years. The tenant then was James J. Morton, a highly respectable councillor and highly thought-of on the Island but too much of a bible-thumper for the likes of us wild laddies as we had to sit still while he read a chapter of the Bible each night. (This wasn't funny when we wanted to swim or play golf). Mrs. Morton was entirely different and a packet of fun - it was her tup lamb

that got me my first ticket back in 1929. One night old James got to the chapter about 'Who begat whom' and as he droned on Mrs M., who was quietly dusting, could stand it no longer and said 'Oh James begat your Auntie'.

I don't know if it's a case of 'The old dog for the hard road' but I've certainly had my share of judging stock this summer. The three Counties at Malvern, the Royal Highland, Fettercairn, Kelso, Nairn, the Black Isle at Muir of Ord and Perth have certainly let me see quite a chunk of the Country; some badly drought ridden, some looking extraordinarily well. When I went north to Nairn and the Black Isle I went over a road that I call the 'roof of Scotland' between Aberfeldy and Dalnacardoch via Trinafour, quite quite lovely even although the purple was bell heather as the real stuff is only just coming out.

As I dropped down at the A9 at Dalnacardoch there was a field of really good sheep-feed rape, not the oil seed stuff one sees everywhere nowadays. I always found rape a more than useful crop as not only did it make a rare job of finishing blackie lambs but their 'golden hooves' left so much goodness in the poorish farms and estates I've managed. This crop I saw certainly looked as if it had had moisture at the right time and I wondered then why in my travels I'd only seen two fields of it.

My judging stints have included Aberdeen-Angus and Highland Cattle and Highland Ponies but by far the most interesting were any other breeds apart from Charolais, Angus, Simmental or Limousin at the Border Union at Kelso.

There were no less than eight other beef breeds - Gelvie, Hereford, Highland, Lincoln Red, Longhorn, Murray Grey, Saler and Shorthorn in alphabetical order. I think these classes are a great idea and should be encouraged at other shows and at the Black Isle, where I was adjudicating among the Highland Cattle, I saw Davie Sinclair sorting out this Heinz 57 variety. I was asked afterwards how you start sorting out these various breeds but to me the first essential is that the beast must be able to walk correctly so that it can graze and get to water, so that it can put on flesh in the right places - ie its backside and top - and hence my champion was the Longhorn cow which was a lovely mover, with flesh as smooth as an apple and nursing a really good calf.

Although a great Highland Cattle enthusiast, I had to give last place in his class to a Highland Bull that had cost a lot of money, this because he couldn't walk and his back as a result looked like the Egyptian Pyramids. The leader in that class was a Saler bull and I hadn't seen many outside their home domain which is the Massif Central in France where they are the equivalent of our Highlands or Galloways: they look useful, but before passing comment I'd like to see how they suckle their calves.

This week I finish my judging stint at Grantown and Kinross but before that I go to Caithness to see an Aberdeen-Angus herd owned by the most gracious lady in the country, whom I will have the honour to meet. No prizes for guessing whom I'm to see.

What *did* we do before the advent of baled silage? These were my thoughts as I travelled from Crieff to Caithness and home via Grantown-on-Spey, then Crieff to Mull and back. There were black bags everywhere. My experience with silage stretched over fifty years to the days in the 1930s when John Brown at Westerton Killearn had a silage tower built which stands to this day. I well remember the tinks who did the labouring for it, Stewarts, I think by name, who were governed by a wizened old crone who one Saturday night, with the drink taken, got hooked up on a barbed wire fence. One of her sons stole the Gladstone bag in which she kept the money and took everywhere with her, and the resulting oaths were hardly music to my ears, brought up as I was in a strict Manse background. We used to fill that tower with a mixture of oats and tares and woe betide anyone trying to get into the tower - because of the gases produced.

Then at Gaskbeg we were told we had to spray our silage with molasses and what a sticky job that was. Next it was draff which in those far off days we got free for the carting - *and* a free dram at the Dalwhinnie Distillery when we uplifted it. And it was salt that we put between each layer as we rolled it in. First class feed it was. Now there are these magnificent bales and surely this year their contents must be excellent altho' in short supply. But, as I've said before, what variations in climate we have in this small Country of ours: although there were black bags of silage in Caithness and Sutherland, there was field after field of rotting hay. How different from the marvellous hay made in so many other areas.

The other thing I couldn't help noticing was how our beef herd has disintegrated. In Speyside no longer did I see fields of Black and Blue Grey cows with tops on them like billiard tables, but instead a mixter maxter of cross continentals. The Continental cattle may have done a great job as terminal sires but not, I fear, as sires of the National Beef Herd.

Apart from one or two herds in Speyside and Caithness and Sutherland I had to go to Mull to see a herd or two of real   cows, one made up of bought-in Blue Greys and the other cross Highland cows by a Whitbread Bull and out of home - bred Highland cows All had really well-milked calves at foot and were a level lot which will give their owners a chance to draw pens of good calves instead of having a job to match them up.

Could it be that the temporary ban on exporting Galloways and Highlanders might give us some more Blue Greys and Highland cows in a year or two's time. After all, they are proven suckler cows.

August

Sally and I have had a real taste of the North-South divide this summer. First was a visit to my old friend John Cridlan, famous along with his father for their string of successes at Smithfield in the carcase competition which they won on countless occasions, culminating in John getting that record price for his champion carcase before he retired. John lived at Remenham and owned all the land beside the hallowed stretch of the Thames where they hold the Henley Regatta which was being held when we stayed with him. By chance his land has been bought by the Copas family of Highland cattle fame who have commercialised the Henley Regatta to their financial advantage. They set up brightly coloured hospitality marquees and lay on everything, catering, nice trailers to take one to a lovely river launch (complete with band and bar) which cruises up the Thames adjacent to the scullers. Our launch was hired from Richard Branson who at that time was ballooning over the Atlantic, and the launch was fabulous.

I have never in all my life seen such opulence and so much money being wasted by so many. The Copas brothers admitted it was the best paying crop they ever grew even although the Regatta only lasts a week. The cars in the car park would make a Scottish farmer who was interested in those sorts of things green with envy, and apart from the latest Range Rovers and Rolls Royces the rest were nearly all bearing the latest registration plates, and mostly foreign. I can see why our trade figures were so bad this summer.

 At the Royal, too, we were surrounded by affluence, noticeable in the car parks, people's dress, but most of all in the shops.

We came home after a sun drenched week to three unmitigated disasters (they always go in threes). Firstly Sal's good mare had torn her leg open on barbed wire. Secondly, the deep freeze had packed in. Thirdly, and worst of all, my croft's two acres of beautiful hay , cut a week , had not even been turned in that gorgeous spell by a young contractor. After a week's continuous rain on my homecoming some super neighbours saved what I call 'fill belly' but couldn't save the grass under the swathes. For all the affluence I encountered in the South I thanked God I was home and I thanked God for good neighbours. What would we do in Scottish farming without them?

September

As I lay in hospital all those many moons ago getting my nose stuck on again and often despairing as one operation succeeded another (all 25 of them), I was always heartened when I looked around to see someone worse off than myself. I felt much the same when I watched the the TV Landward programme on the state of New Zealand farming. We think we're badly off in some areas but we don't start compared with their plight. I wonder where we would be now if we hadn't joined the E E C. Without the drought on the Continent I don't think barley would be making £130 a ton. Which may not solve the future grain mountain but at least it should keep a few bank managers happy.

In an effort to diversify, one New Zealand farmer had gone in for trees - and hard-woods at that. I feel this is something we should be thinking about very carefully. Why can't a crop of timber be valued at a tenant's waygoing just as with any other crop? I know there would need to be alterations to the Agricultural Holdings Act but that surely is within the realms of possibility. There is no doubt we need more timber and I'm fed up with those thousands of acres of blanket Sitka Spruce owned by faceless Sassanachs who have them only for a tax wangle.

Then another diversification are horses. Thanks to TV coverage and Royal patronage, horses are a boom industry in this country and eat a lot of our produce and employ many thousands of people, apart from giving endless healthy pleasure to many more thousands. Some farmers are thinking seriously of giving over some of their old steadings as horse boxes and grazing some horses for a welcome bit of extra cash. Then there are others, mostly in the Southern Counties who breed and train National Hunt horses and we in Scotland can be proud of names like the Callant, Wynburgh, Merryman II, Lucius, Earlsbrig and many many others. And it has been a joy to see young Peter Dunn, back virtually from death, with a smile like a rising sun, leading in his winner at Perth Races. All power to the likes of him who not only afford many thousands their pleasure but also integrate it with farming.

I can never decide which produces more aggro, a Kirk Session meeting or the greetin' meetin' of an Agricultural Show. I ought to have found out by now as I've attended both for over 30 years. We had the latter last week of the Ardoch Agricultural Society and there was less aggro than I've ever known in all the different Show Societies with which I've been associated.

77

September

Even the Steward of the afternoon parade and the Chief Horse Steward saw eye to eye on moving some rings about, absolutely unprecedented. The reason - for once we had a wonderful sunny day and had made a profit. Two things have changed dramatically in the show accounts over the years: one is sponsorship (unheard of until recently) and the other is trade stands. I always thought trade stands at local shows were only there to fly the flag and to water their customers so I was amazed, when having a 'refresh' on the stand of a well known estate agent, actually to hear someone wanting to buy a farm. And they tell me that a new tractor was sold on a machinery stand at Braco. Great news indeed and obviously the stand holders must think their rents are justified. As for our ice cream man, for once he did a roaring trade, but the hamburger man not so well.

Many shows are going to have a job to survive financially and I've no doubts that shows that have committees, who don't employ contractors but do the work themselves, who go out for sponsorship and who let their stand space prudently will be the survivors.

I had reason to attend a Highland funeral during the past fortnight in a typically hill area of Inverness-shire. Sal and I as two of the principal mourners were out of the church in the van of the congregation and I was able to study the faces of the people as they came out. There was character stamped on each and every one, both male and female, and it set me wondering what had done it. Was it the climate with its long cold hard winters - for spring comes late up there. As they were all farming stock, was it the hard unremitting toil of the 1930s and 1940s before mechanisation and electricity helped them out (they were all of the older generation) or was it that every penny was needed and they were canty with it? Whatever it was, these were faces of people with whom all us farming folk should be proud to be associated. As should we be with the elderly lady, of farming stock, a great show attender, who at Braco this year had her arm broken when a steer, quite accidentally and through nobody's fault, slipped and rolled on her arm. This lovely lady, when sent flowers from the show committee, replied in a letter, by return, saying how the flowers had brightened her day. She was effusive in her thanks. No word of claims, just thanks. We in the farming world should be proud that we still have the salt of the earth among us.

September

I dearly love the story of the two Aberdeenshire farm loons who were called up during the last war and were serving in the Western Desert amidst the sand and flies and under the scorching sun. Sandy turned to Jock and said 'Fit day is it?'. 'Goad man it's the first Tuesday o' August. Turra Show day'. Sandy looking up at the blazing sun set in the cloudless sky replied 'Man there're gettin' a braw day for't'

September

Well perhaps Scots farming folk on holiday on the Costa Brava or the Greek Islands this summer may have been saying the same thing but most shows including Turra were well nigh washed out. But showing stock is a disease and it would take more than a wet day to dissuade that hardy and happy band.

This year I was called on to judge at various shows from the prestigious Royal to the Great Yorkshire to a super wee show in Kilmuir in the North tip of Skye. All shows have different characteristics but all play a major part in our farming calendar.

My first show was the Fife County Show - for which that great character, the late Charlie Drummond, did so much. The weather wasn't too good there and the field was wet.

I was judging the Highland Ponies and took great pleasure in putting up the ridden class winner as my overall champion. This mare of Heather Turnbull's went on to have a great season and I think was unbeaten in the Highland ridden class. But you can't please everyone and one disgruntled exhibitor (who incidentally is both a great pal of mine and unbeatable on the fiddle) said 'Ben couldn't judge combines'. Actually he's right on that score.

Then it was off to the Royal where the ponies ware judged on the Thursday and we had the only really hot day I've experienced all summer, I'm sorry to say the Highland Ponies were not as good as I would have hoped. But I'm told that when I go South to judge the Highland pony enthusiasts' club in Sussex I'll get a good turnout. Compared with the Royal the Great Yorkshire is compact and very friendly and everyone talks about 'our show'. When I first went there it was the first show I'd seen that had free car parking - the late Matt Balwin's brain child. He was ex-Black Watch and an excellent secretary. To this day the show is more generous to Breed Societies and Breed Society Secretaries than any other.

But I was there to judge the Highland cattle and I couldn't help remembering the early days of those classes at this show when the late Pearson Brown caused ever so many Scots to cross the Border and show their cattle at Harrogate. Pearson got ever so many folds started in Yorkshire and as a butcher used nothing but Highland beef. As a result he had an extremely discerning clientele. He was proud of the fact that he was the only person who had a Highland steer in the final line-up of four at the Smithfield Show. And he still is. I once heard him lecturing to a bunch of cattlemen about handling beef and he said that the day before an animal was slaughtered it should be left absolutely quiet as stress during that 24 hours was the reason for a lot of tough meat. This I have proved: we tried to chase a stag at Blackmount out of a plantation and after chasing it for half a day we eventually had to shoot. The resulting venison was so tough we had to throw it away.

I am Chairman of the Ardoch Show, and after a week of rain, and three inches on the day before, every cattle float had to be pulled in and out of the showground. But the weather was so bad everyone was moaning about it and for once I never heard a murmur against the judges.

The trip to Skye was through torrential rain and the person judging the ponies had to run them out on a peat bog. I was luckier as I had the local mart in which to judge, even if it was open to elements. I had 120 good cattle in all, none haltered and my first class was of 20 cows and calves at foot to be judged as pairs. Not easy.

Dalmally, a great favourite of mine was last Saturday, and what a transformation has come over their sheep classes. Gone are the fuzzie-headed long woolled brutes, and hill farms are showing stock worthy of many a tup breeder.

How we all love the social side of our shows, and none more than those in the remoter areas. With past experience I took Sally as driver to Skye. I needn't have bothered as there was no beer tent and as I quaffed my glass of water with the excellent lunch, Sally was convulsed and said 'That'll be a shock to your system'. I doot the Wee Frees have a lot to answer for.

I have heard two very interesting radio programmes recently. (I nearly said wireless programmes but my girls tease me when I use that word saying 'Dad, the days of crystal sets and cats whiskers went out with the ark'). The first programme was Ian Grant, our N F U President, explaining, as only he can, to the urban population who are the main audience listening to the

September

'Head On' Programme what set-aside would do to the countryside as we know it, and telling them in the nicest possible way that if everyone took it up and if we entirely forsook all nitrogen and stopped all spraying we would be heading for dearer, scarcer food. No scaremongering, just good commonsense, middle of the road arguments. It set me thinking how lucky we are to have people like Ian to represent our industry, and yet funnily enough I know of some of our ablest farmers, who have done financially well from the work done by the Union, who are frequently bashing it, and some aren't even members of it.

Then there was a programme on the Countryside chaired by Vic Robertson of 'The Scotsman'. He had people from different backgrounds expressing how they felt the land should be owned and run. My heart warmed to the landlord who wanted to leave his estate in better nick that when he inherited it. He was already diversified in many directions but he was the first to admit that he owned a sand and gravel quarry, which they tell me is the best 'dreepin' roast' a farmer could have.

On the same programme was an M P, representing a town constituency, who was adamant that we were all ruining the countryside, that modern farming methods were all wrong etc - all the old false arguments that get trundled out by people who don't deal direct with nature and have never had to make a living from the land and think we are all barley barons who rip out the hedges. And as Ian Grant said he can't think of any hedges at all that have been ripped out in his neck of the woods.

There's no doubt we're under siege - in one day in my local paper there were two lots of 'Anti's'. One was anti testing on animals and the other, headed by Pamela Stephenson who is mother of Billy Connolly's children, was calling on all farmers to stop spraying their crops as she reckoned that a generation of 'chemical children' were being raised for the sake of farmers' profits. All I can say to Pamela Stephenson is, if she has any more children she'll be needing more food to keep them going - and in her way of things, feeding them will be gey expensive.

At the date of the Killin suckled calf sale, the swallows go, and the Greylag geese are honking overhead - all sure signs of approaching winter and still the bulk of the harvest to be 'safely gathered in'.

September

I was down in my second favourite County last week to judge Highland ponies and that County is Sussex, where I spent three years of my early life and in whose County Regiment I served during the war.

Perthshire of course takes pride of place in my book, as it has everything, the Weald of Scotland my father called it. When I was travelling overseas either on my lecture tours (for the English Speaking Union or the International Wool Secretariat) or when I was representing the Aberdeen-Angus overseas, which I did in ten countries, the highlight of my trip was always breasting the hill in Glendevon and seeing Strathearn unfolding in front of me. The mixture is so breath taking with its patchwork quilt of the mixed farming of the Strath, certainly more predominant arable than it used to be - more's the pity - its lovely stands of timber and the heather covered backcloth of the Turret hills to the North. I used literally to thank God that Strathearn is my home.

What has caused this eulogy is the quite unjustified outcry by the do-gooders about how we farmers are bespoiling the countryside. What a lot of twaddle. The view from Duncton ring on the South Downs in Sussex is much the same as it was when I used to ride exercise all those fifty years ago. What has changed are the number of arterial roads and motorways, the huge concourse of Gatwick Airport taking up hundreds of acres of good arable land where once there was a little steeplechase race course, almost as scenic as Perth. Down the road from it they were building yet another vast supermarket with parking for 1,000 cars. These are the people who are despoiling the lovely Sussex countryside as are the so called planners who have taken over the South coast since the war and if that's planning, thank God we in farming plan our farms better even if some of our buildings leave a lot to be desired from an aesthetic point of view.

My thoughts about how we farmers (with but a few exceptions) are doing more than most for conservation have been more aptly summed up than ever I could do it by James Hunter in 'Agribusiness'. For those who don't get this excellent farming journal, (one of the better ones of the endless stream of farming bumph that cascades through one's letterbox) he says the trouble is that the British and especially the English because of the Industrial revolution want to see the countryside as they reckon it should be, with farm workers in smocks, horse drawn hay wains, and us farmers sucking straws. And he is so right when he says that if we were still farming as they did a century ago and got a year like this one, there would be really hardship for the whole country.

No matter how one tries one just can't get away from the weather. On an estate I managed, where stalking plays a major part of the economy, the weather has been so appalling and the mist so constant that only a fifth of the normal stags have been shot. As for the sheep fanks you'd think you'd rolled the lambs on the floor after they'd been drawn. Well, I suppose it'll all get sorted out in the end and young men today will tell their grand children about the terrible summers they once knew. As an old farmer once said to me when I was coming my lay preacher stuff about the Lord always giving us a seed time and harvest, he said 'Aye but the Lord never said *when*'.

October

I suppose it must be over a quarter of a century ago. I was coming back from Mull to Oban on the old steamer, the 'Lochinvar', it was one of those warm Indian summer days that we can get in October and on the deck was a pile of red deer carcases - stags, hinds and calves and buzzing round them were a host of bluebottles. I was shocked that hinds and calves had been killed at that time of the year but even more shocked when I saw this pile of rubbish, because that's what it was, being collected by someone whom I thought to be a reputable game dealer. No wonder venison got a bad name.

But luckily all that has changed. Deer forest owners, stalkers and game dealers have made great strides in presentation of their venison and now demand far outstrips supply. I believe that, given the right sort of farm, deer farming is the diversification I would go for were I still in farming. This was borne out when I was in New Zealand where they couldn't understand why we hadn't more deer farmers producing farmed venison, for they, the New Zealanders, are sending us something like 50,000 carcases a year or roughly half our present total demand, which is bound to grow, as do the shouts from my least favourite Antis, the Anti-this, anti-that, and anti the next food lobby that may in their minds have been produced unhealthily. With the demand for breeding hinds at £600 a piece it's no wonder only the farmed stags worth £150 to £250 have found their way onto the market leaving the shortfall that is being filled by New Zealand.

As with every new venture, one needs to learn about it, work hard at it and have sufficient capital to fund it - not so easy these days.

It's also a quarter of a century ago that anyone who was farming organically was the laughing stock of the industry, and known as the 'muck and magic' farmer. Changed days indeed as the consumers are demanding more and more organically produced vegetables, yes, and milk and beef in certain areas. I was in a local veg shop the other day and the lady in front of me said she wouldn't buy any more potatoes (as the last she had bought were tasteless) until the shopkeeper got some organically grown ones. But will those wishing organically produced food pay more? Ah, there's the rub, as Will Shakespeare said.

I for one was a great believer in muck and still get my Golden Wonders from a farmer that uses plenty of it. It's strange how certain farmers laughed at the old Scottish practice of feeding cattle in a court saying the cattle only

85

gave the farmer the pleasure of their company in exchange for their winter's keep. It's also strange that in this district at any rate you can tell the farms that spread dung and plough in grass. They've got hidden capital. When I was a boy we used to say what looks like manure smells like manure but sounds like the village bell? Dung. Great stuff!

When I worked for the late Michael Noble when he was Secretary of State for Scotland there was nothing that relaxed him more, from that very exacting job, than standing around a piano with a glass in his hand singing the songs of the North, of which he knew the lot. One of his favourites was 'The Bush above Traquair' which says, 'As you hear the cooshies croon on a gowden afternoon on the high Minch Moor you're up and awa'. It was to that high Minch Moor that I took Sally one of those fabulous days that we've been enjoying recently.

We went on into Yarrow and Ettrick, where I had only been once since shepherding in that lovely valley all those years ago. What changes I saw, and not all for the better.

Gone were the gairs on which we spent so much time in the old pre-war days. For those who don't know what a gair is, one starts with a spring - and springs abound on most hill farms - and digs a drain with a rutting spade at an angle down hill allowing the water to seep out down the hill at the end of it. The next year you extend the drain so that another area is irrigated and so on, with the result that you have green patches all along the hillside reminiscent of that startling green one associated with ground around a spring.

But all I saw this year were those abominable huge drains carving a hillside to bits so that my abomination the Sitka spruce could be planted. Why can't we integrate Forestry and Farming? But thank God for those lovely-faced South Country Cheviots (with their mothering ability) which have stood the Borders in such good stead. I did enjoy seeing them and the few herds of true Blue Grey cows which are a joy to behold instead of the mixter maxter of breeds that make up a so-called breeding herd these days. I'm always hoping that the rise in overheads will turn people back to our native breeds and crosses and to the breeding herd using a continental bull as the terminal sire. The Irish also think along the same lines judging by their excellent display of heifers at Perth last week. Perhaps this awful crunch we are

October

getting in farming will make some folk realise that big is not always beautiful.

My favourite Psalm is 121. To those who are not 'kirk greedy' the first two lines read, 'I to the hills will lift mine eyes from whence doth come mine aid'. The cynics among you will be saying 'Old Ben's thinking of the aid he got from the Hill Farming Act Scheme', of which more later. But they'd be wrong. No! it's their steadfastness, their changing beauty, snow-capped in winter, green in the spring, heather purple in the summer and in autumn russet brown, that's what never ceases to enchant me. Also it's their challenge, and challenges I've always liked. I've spent a lot of my working life challenging them, reseeding and draining in Glenlochay Killin in the late 1940s, killing bracken (again becoming what Naomi Mitchinson called one of the three Bs that blighted the Highlands - Braxy, Bracken and McBraynes). It was bracken killing along with proper Muir Burn I did at

87

October

Gaskbeg in the 1950s, then to Ardkinglas and Blackmount in the 1960s and 1970s where one had to fight against the 100 plus inches of rain with its frightening resulting spates making fencing, draining and road making a constant battle.

But during this past fortnight I've had two lovely but sad days in my beloved hills. Firstly as back-up man to Sal and two of her friends who were riding their Highland Ponies from Linn of Dee through Glen Tilt to Blair Atholl. Having dropped them off on Deeside on a lovely autumn morning I arranged to meet them above Blair at between 4.30 and 5.00 pm. Four came, then half past, then five, half past and then six, so fearing the worst I set off up Glen Tilt and that's where the sad bit came in. No nothing had come over the riders - only a pony had cast a shoe and the going had been rocky. I was, however, passing acre after acre of lovely hill grass blowing in the wind and not a mouth on it and by the time the stags came down to graze it the frost will have nicked it.

Then the next week I had a day's stalking on my beloved Blackmount, at 73 no longer on the high tops (so well written up by one of the Lady Breadalbanes in 'The High Tops of Blackmount') and once again I saw remains of clachans that would be summer grazing of old. What tales these stones could tell! It set me thinking why is it that a country like Switzerland can subsidise its small hill farmers, living from 1,600 to 6,000 ft above sea level, to the tune of £7,000 per head (and more) and yet we in this hopelessly overpopulated country of ours let these old shielings go completely unused?

The Hill Farming Act was a step in the right direction. It was a comprehensive scheme, and one couldn't just install electricity in the farmer's house or do up the farm road, you had to do the lot - dipper, fank, fencing, lime and slag etc. It seems criminal that we're not doing more for the 'hills from whence doth come our aid' because the hills have bred both men and stock that have done a lot for British Agriculture. Yes for Britain - I know I'm getting sentimental in my old age but of one thing I'm certain - the Good Lord isn't going to make us any more land especially after the way we've treated some of it already.

For my money we are heading for a worse clearance of the Highlands than was ever seen all those years ago. Why worse? Because then there were too many people for the land to sustain. But now we have all too few people in our hills and uplands and everything should be done to keep those who are there.

When my late boss Duncan Stewart, along with many far sighted politicians of the 1940s (and there aren't many far-sighted ones around today) formulated the 1947 Agricultural Act, the hill sheep and cow subsidies were built in more as a social subsidy than anything else. But now we have the E.E.C. talking of phasing out the sheep variable premium, which has been hinted at for some time. But the crunch is that it would be substituted by a ewe premium for all breeding ewes, hill and arable alike.

I know arable farmers will say 'There goes Old Ben beating the hill farmer's drum again'. I do quite unashamedly as, having had a foot in both camps, I know that the arable farmer can diversify, more today than ever, and in most cases should be fattening hill and upland lambs before the glut comes on. The hill man can't diversify and an overall ewe subsidy, with modern practices of inoculations, in wintering, etc available to the arable farmer, will flood the market, and our next mountain will be one of lamb while the mountains of Scotland will be taken over by the climbers and hill walkers leaving their plastic litter as they go.

The plight of the people who inhabit our lonely areas was brought home to me when I was talking to two stalkers' wives when I attended an Estate ceilidh last weekend. I have known the two families for a quarter of a century and seen the young grow up into fine teenagers. They are the sort of people who breed the lads and lassies o' pairts that have made Scotland so famous around the world. Both families have members who have made University where they find they are ostracised because of their inability to play all the games that seem to be the in-thing nowadays like rugger, hockey, squash, tennis, volleyball etc. Is this the advent of TV or the fact that sporting personalities are set on pedestals and paid far too much money?

Whatever the reason, these two super mothers, who have made a great job of rearing nice families, said that if they had their lives to live over again they wouldn't live in the Highlands. To me the hill and upland folk are the life blood of our country and we lose the folk who belong there at our peril. Everyone in places of authority should be trying to support and strengthen life in the hills. If nothing is done to help the Highlanders we'll be engulfed by White Settlers.

It was music to my ears when I heard in one of the sale reports that a pen of Cross Highlanders in calf to an Aberdeen-Angus bull had topped the Stirling in-calf-heifer sale. Gone are the days when one saw pen upon pen of good Cross Highland heifers in Dingwall, Oban and Stirling. And judging by the number of Aberdeen-Angus bulls in Perth this week they are going to be in short supply as well unless there is a complete turn-around.

The only people who could reverse the trend would be the consumers of beef. Not that I'm saying continental bulls don't produce good beef. But it's the cow herd that worries me. We depend more and more on the dairy herd for our beef and in all too many cases for our hill cow replacements, so our beef gets less and less tasty. I was interested to read an article the other day which stated quite categorically that farmers and butchers had only themselves to blame for the falling off of demand for beef, because they were breeding the wrong sort of cattle and because they didn't hang their beef. The writer said that she knew of two butchers who were doing a roaring trade, one in a London suburb who sold nothing but Angus beef and one in Devon who sold nothing but Devon beef, the famous Red Rubies. There was no mention in her article of the much vaunted Continentals, but because of the type of farming we are now in I'm sure they are here to stay. One just wonders what is the next fad and fashion we'll see and if there are any more breeds to import. I suppose we could always introduce the Yak, but looking at some of today's so-called 'modern' cattle perhaps some countries have used them already. I was one of the people who was against the importation of the Simmental and had a running pen battle on the subject with the late Sir Wm. Young of the Scottish Farmer.

How wrong I've been proved. They have done a great job in many areas but I'm sad that they have been included in the Islands heifer rearing scheme. With hay already at £100 per ton delivered in Mull, surely the Department of Agriculture and the West of Scotland College should be advocating breeds that are economic to feed. The most avid Simmental supporter - and I'm thinking of Charlie Allan especially - could scarcely advocate that a cross Simmental would be as easy to feed as say a Blue Grey or a cross Highlander. And what happens to our replacement stocks if we use the Simmental as the first cross sire and not the terminal sire? I think this has been a bad piece of leadership from the Department when they could have saved our native breeds that have been proved over countless years as sound foundation stock for our hills and Islands.

I had a dead hogg the other day. When the knackery man came for it he obviously wanted a bit crack and as we slung the hogg on board I saw he had five cows on board. 'Staggers?' I asked 'Aye, four of them are, and within a ten mile radius of you.' No wonder the price of in-calf heifers is so high. 'But what about the fifth?' I asked. 'Oh! she is the fourth cow I've collected from the same farm with calving problems, so the farmer is getting rid of his continental bull and going to Perth to buy an Angus'. Music to a believer's ears.

The tattie holidays have come and gone once more. In fact only a fraction of school children now go tattie howkin. No longer are thousands of Scottish school children dependent on the tattie money for their winter boots and clothes, as they were in the past. The holidays stay mainly to break up that long winter term from August until Christmas.

October

The other day I was talking to a well known potato merchant and he was saying that half the pleasure has gone out of the lifting time for him with the advent of the lifting machines. No more does he get the jokes with the howkers or the horrors of seeing his squad disappear over the nearest dyke on the advent of the DHSS man out to check on those that were drawing 'the buroo'. I was telling him of the balmy days forty years ago when I used to go to Raploch in Stirling in an old ex-army lorry and there were so many volunteers that I could choose my squad. Then there were the German Prisoners of War, all ex-farm workers and first class pickers. Ah! memory hold the door!

For all its faults the Potato Marketing Board have done a damned good job. Thanks to their control the potato crop hasn't gone through the roof in acreage as have so many other crops. This is all the more commendable when one thinks of the tonnages we can now achieve with our new techniques and varieties - although to my taste I would as soon eat soap as some of them. There are constant complaints of blackleg and ground keepers. I can't see why the first should be   such a worry but as for the second to my simple mind it's just a matter of bad farming. One never found a ground keeper when one had a decent rotation and even if one can't afford a seven course shift any more one can surely have some grass somewhere instead of having white crop succeeding white crop and giving the keepers every opportunity of continual growth.

Surely the Marketing Board's biggest fault is its vast expenditure on administration - something like three quarters of its income, if not more. This is a country-wide disease, worse than beef roll and mosaic put together, but one the Board should tackle *pronto.*

The Board monitors the potato acreage when necessary by photos taken from a helicopter. I feel the only way we can get out of our grain mountain situation is to have compulsory fallowing programme monitored by photos. It would do the land good on many overcropped farms and if done proportionately the big boys would be curtailed as well. Of course there would have to be recompense but surely it wouldn't cost any more than storing unwanted grain, and we'd be keeping land in better fettle for the day when it was required again.

November

When my father was unsuccessfully trying to dissuade me from entering farming, on the bottom rung of the ladder, way back in the early 1930s he used to sing a song that he picked up during his service in the First World War. It went, 'How you going to get them back on the farm now that they've seen Paree?' This catchy tune kept repeating itself to me when I spent a fortnight in Paphos in Cyprus because that's one of the big problems there. The youth of the countryside have tasted the flesh pots of Paphos and don't want to go 'back on the farm now that they've seen Paphos'.

My old boss Sir James Roberts bought property out there when building land was under £100 an acre, but when Cyprus was divided in 1974 and the Greek Taverna owners came down from the North, Paphos with its harbour, beaches, mosaics, ruins and a history that stretches back to 1500 BC, made an obvious tourist centre and now with its international airport land is worth tens of thousands of pounds an acre. And of course the local farming community has benefited in some ways and lost in others. The locals are fearfully worried about the future of the poorer and smaller farms (where have we heard that story before?) and most of the vineyards and orange groves are being worked by an ageing community or by part-time farmers. It was one of the latter who befriended Sally and myself. He was Sergeant in the local Police Force. He very kindly gave up his day off to take us out to his vineyard and orange grove. The vines were of course stripped of their fruit at this time of the year and his grapes go to the local Co-operative where they are made into excellent and cheap wine. He uses contract labour to harvest his crop and as it is a chauvinistic country the men get £5 per day more than the women. The oranges on the other hand were just ripening and he had just sprayed them against some bugs or other. He said that without sprays and fertilisers he couldn't compete with either of his crops on the world market (there's nothing new in this world) and judging by the taste of the tatties they must use an awful lot of fertiliser on them. But they are grown on the good land east of Paphos, three crops a year and a highly organised industry at that.

The Sergeant used a wee tractor for his cultivation and sighed for the days when he kept a donkey. It had fed on a bit of straw and grass, it had cost a mere £50, lived for 20 years and didn't need a licence, petrol or maintenance and never broke down.

The only thing I don't like about that friendly Island is the number of scrounging cats of which there are dozens just waiting to slip in the apartment door. Some bear the mark of Coutts' size twelves on their bottoms.

We have just had our Church Harvest Thanksgiving. We have always believed that all should be 'safely gathered in' before it is held, although one minister we had, who was a Canadian, said it didn't matter when it was held as somewhere in the world someone would be harvesting.

How things have changed since my first harvest thanksgiving when the church was full of sheaves of corn. And around Glasgow in those days oats was the only cereal crop grown. The vegetables, too, were tatties and neeps and a few apples. But with the entry into the Common Market and the awareness of different varieties of vegetables it is nothing unusual to find peppers, courgettes, sprouting broccoli etc on display.

Another big difference is when it comes to dispensing the harvest gifts. Back in my schoolboy days we were in the middle of the real Depression of the late 1920s and early 1930s, when there were scores of families who were really hard up and were glad of a bit extra. Now we find most of our OAPs are better off and they are not on the bread line as they were back then.

One cynic said to me 'What are we having a harvest thanksgiving for this year?' I'm afraid my reply was swift and cutting when I said 'Have you ever seen a volcano erupt or experienced a hurricane? Have you ever seen snow the height of the fences last for six months? All right, we had a wet summer and things are going to be tough but we did get in a harvest of sorts and we've had some right good years in farming since the War'. He didn't answer but I made my point on a subject on which I have *very* strong views. After all, no one asked us to farm, I never wanted to do anything else. But if we do farm we have to put up with the vagaries of the weather and with the way that nature plays its part. We must just go along with them and not fight against them.

Another thought I had at the Harvest Thanksgiving was what a strong lobby there is for No Additives. In the old days jars of jam, sauce etc had (in very small print) the additives which the food contained but now *in large print* many foods have No Additives. This lobby is getting stronger and stronger and we dismiss it at our peril.

The no hormone brigade are becoming vociferous and I am one, not because I'm against what they might do to me at more than three score year and ten, but because anything that puts people off eating meat is a bad thing. These folk are the tip of the iceberg and younger farmers will need to woo future consumers as never before.

Going back to my sceptical pal, I told him it was a good thing we didn't have a referendum on the weather as we'd have a drought every year. Whereas the Lord gets it about right most years.

I have recently been frequenting different Marts selling Blackmount lambs, ewes and rams and a rattling good trade we got. The lambs from this Estate have to be sold later than do many hill farms because the head shepherd is also a first class stalker and is needed until the middle of October. This year it paid off as our wether lambs and our ewes topped the market. But what a gamble we farmers have to put up with. Many a year when it's a good early harvest our sheep would have been sold too late in the season after arable farmers had got filled up.

November

These thoughts prompted me to ponder on the Words of Abraham Lincoln which were read out to me by an old friend of mine whom I met at one of the sheep sales. It goes like this:-

'If one day the cities disappear the fields will survive but if the fields disappear the cities will not survive'.

How true, but you wouldn't think so the way we're being chivvied from pillar to post by every anti-lobby that ever was, including our Minister of Agriculture and the Government that control him.

Funny how we are the darlings of the country when the threat of war is imminent, but I suppose having gone forty years since the last one we've been lucky that by and large we've been well paid for our efforts and we've become too darned efficient. Or have we? I shudder to think what some farmers must be paying in the way of interest on their overdrafts. I fear some college advisory men, fertiliser manufacturers, unpleasant salesmen and bank managers will have quite a lot to answer for if the bankruptcies that are expected in farming materialise.

When I factored Millhills forty years ago, we had a tenant who wished to retire and at the roup you never saw such a load of old but workable implements, mostly horse drawn but some converted to be pulled by his one and only grey Ferguson tractor (of blessed memory). He didn't even have a binder as he borrowed the Laird's. As a young factor, I pulled his leg about the antiquity of his tackle and he replied, 'Laddie, I never knew a farmer mak' money out of concrete or new implements'. Need I say he died a very wealthy man.

The late Lovat Fraser (that prince of auctioneers) when I asked him for an overdraft of £700 to go into Gaskbeg said 'Yes, as long as you have a herd of cattle and a flock of sheep: should things go wrong you'll have something to sell'. How true to this day and it's only a terrible shame that so many of the good quality beef hind quarters are going into intervention and so much of our cross dairy rubbish comes onto the home market because that is one of the many reasons why some people have turned against meat eating. They are no longer getting the class of beef that is tender and tasty. Because of the beef mountain we in Scotland who have been famous for generations for producing quality beef are no longer being encouraged to rear that beef in our hills and uplands to be fattened on our arable farms.

November

If only we could get back to being a stock-rearing country - apart from that golden strip round our east coast - a lot of our difficulties would fade away. But how does one turn back the clock? I return to Abraham Lincoln: 'If the fields disappear the cities will not survive!' And the 'fields' mean all of us, big farmers, hill farmers, dairy farmers, crofters, the lot.

In the old days when there was no television, that curse of all social occasions, hill sheep deliveries were great occasions. I have just been at a hill sheep delivery and naturally my thoughts turned back to when I took over the sheep stock at Gaskbeg about forty years ago. Although there were only 500 ewes to take over - and in the end it turned out there were a mere 350 counted - forty people attended just to see how good, or in this case bad, the stock were.

Sheep deliveries have had a great part to play in the Highlands. It is said that the once influential and wealthy Campbells of Breadalbane were bankrupted not only because they 'lived it up' but also because they had to pay vast sums to tenant farmers for the acclimatisation of their ewe stocks. It's frightening to think that once 'from Kenmore to Ben More the land is a' the Marquis's'. The Ben More being in Mull and the Marquis was the Marquis of Breadalbane. The family now own nothing.

The sheep deliveries could be fairly contentious. The Laird appointed one valuator and the tenant another and then they had an oversman to see fair play. The sums paid in the 1920s, when one thinks of inflation, were astronomic. Just after the last War all farms that had used the Hill Farming Act, that super scheme that did so much for us in the hills, had to be valued under the Act, which took an average of five years of the cast ewe price plus so much for acclimatisation, and from memory I think so much for younger ages. This brought in the era of single valuers as the whole job has some guidelines. But the whole delivery job is the same. The sheep have to be gathered and held so that they can be counted and the shotts (or bad sheep) culled by the valuer. The in going and out going farmers, be they Lairds or tenants, have to sign a submission drawn up by a lawyer as the basis of the valuation. The practicalities are also the same, one squad helping the valuer discard the shotts, and one man counting for the ingoer and one for the outgoer apart from the valuer's clerk who also counts, making trebly certain the count is correct.

Then there is a second squad dosing and inoculating, and a third dipping the ewes and keeling them as any that come in unkeeled at the next gathering will have to be paid for. Last week as of old the hospitality was immense, 1,200 ewes were taken over compared with fewer that 400 all those years ago, and instead of 40 people there were a mere 16.

The Islands of Capri and Mull have tourism in common but little else. In one respect they differ enormously and that is when the mist enshrouds Capri as it did every morning we were there. It meant we were in for a hot day whereas in Mull I would think it meant rain.

Like all Mediterranean and Asiatic Islands, being volcanic, Capri had little available arable land and they make the most of it, growing vegetables, olives, grapes and flowers - the latter in profusion and graveyards are awash with them. If I'm to be reincarnated I'd plump for being a florist in Capri!

The worst invention for this Island was the combustion engine. There are lovely flagged-stoned, narrow donkey roads all over the Island and they are now taken over by motor bikes and wee 3-wheeled trucks being driven by speed crazed Italians.

I met a Canadian farmer on the trip who was bemoaning the fact that his country was fast losing their small farmers, with disastrous results to the future of Canada. So we're not the only country with that problem. Then there was an English farmer who told me that on his 2,000 acres the hedges had been decimated - the first person I've ever met who has actually done what we so often only hear about. He also told me how he produced thousands of tons of potatoes that were tasteless but as they had shallow eyes and scrubbed up well and made him a big profit all was right with the world. I sometimes despair of my fellow farmers who abandon the quality ship.

After Capri it was Sorrento where the olive harvest was in full swing, the olives being collected in nets hung under the trees to prevent bruising. I was amazed to learn that it takes five kilos of olives to make one litre of olive oil. No wonder it's expensive. Although we never saw a cattle beast

outside there was a big cheese factory which we visited where they made Mozzarella which is used in all their farinaceous dishes, and delicious they were. But the cheese makers were bemoaning the fact that the cow keepers were packing up as they found milking the tourists much more profitable.

A lot of farming correspondents love to dip into Europe and return to tell us what we'll be up against in 1992. But agriculturally a visit to Sorrento would be a waste of their time - unless they wanted a wine tasting tour.

I have a faded photo in my album of which I am very proud. It shows Sergeant-Major Coutts ploughing with a pair of oxen in Abyssinia (now Ethiopia) back in 1940. Kassala, which is often mentioned as the starting point for the long haul of food supplies was the spot from which our guns fired the opening shot in the campaign all those 50 years ago. What saddens me is that it is once more War that is disrupting the distribution of these much needed supplies.

When we were there the economy was a peasant one and even with a War raging around them the native people, mostly super hill men, were ploughing, sowing, and reaping. Now, thanks to Civil War *and* successive droughts, they are starving. Surely there is something very far wrong when we are being made to set aside acres of good productive land in a country with the greatest agricultural expertise in the world when millions are dying. Eastern Europe, too, will be a long time before it gets its agricultural act together and I'll bet will need food for the foreseeable future. It's a topsy turvy world, and always has been.

I've just finished the biography of the Duchess of Atholl *Katherine Atholl* by S J Hetherington. The Duchess was M P for the old Kinross and West Perth constituency from 1928-38. When I was a boy at St. Fillans she was known as the 'Red Duchess' because of her leanings towards the Communists in the Spanish Civil War.

And in the early 1930s she was one of the few far-sighted M Ps who fore saw the menace of Hitler. She was ousted in a bye-election by Wm (later Sir Wm) McNair Snadden who was to be a boss of mine in the late 1940s. But the interesting thing on reading the account of that bye-election is that is was the *farming* vote that unseated the Duchess. It set me wondering in how many constituencies could that happen today?

When one thinks of the M Ps that we've had since the War with either active farming experience or a farming background - like McNair Snadden, Gomme Duncan, the Mackie brothers, Tony Stoddart, Michael Noble etc - now one has to do quite a bit of scratching around to find two or three in the whole House of Commons. And what farmers are there from Scotland to air our views today? Even the N F U will have difficulties filling their top jobs as farmers are having to do more and more of their own work - and the 'bumph' work is not getting any easier.

I was up getting a truck load of hay for the ponies from my good friend and neighbour. He tied the load down with that well known knot, beloved of every good horse or tractorman for securing a load, I was never very good at it, but I can tie a cattle beast or a horse with the slip knot that would hold a battleship but can be loused with one pull. Nowadays all the big loads have patent straps on them so the art of knot tying is going to be lost. As are many other country arts. Only the other day I had to show a town lassie, who was mucking out a horse box, that a graip is bent upwards so one turns it upside down to let go the dung.

December

A well known whisky advert reads 'Quality in an age of change'. I only wish the same thing could be said about farming, where I'm afraid it's a case of 'Quantity in an age of change', and goodness what quantities and what changes - with a record harvest, especially of winter cereals and our tatties selling at give-away prices. And the housewife buying one fifth less meat than she did four years ago. Is it not high time we in the industry as a whole took a damned good look at ourselves and found out what our modern housewives really want? For too long we have been inclined to think that the world owes us a living.

It was with these thoughts in my head that I set off to the Smithfield Show. I first attended it at Earls Court in 1949 when I showed a Highland bullock and some cross hoggs for the late Duncan Stewart, the bullock was a three year old and the hoggs were of course a year older than we would show today, So in that period of time we have changed. This was brought about by pressure from the wholesale butchers on our Council, telling us our stock was too fat, so first the sheep section inaugurated a live-dead competition whereby animals were judged live and then as carcase. The cattle section joined suit and now the Show has changed dramatically. But are we producing quality?

I little thought as a farm manager back in '49, that I would gain the exalted position of being one of the Vice-Presidents of the prestigious Royal Smithfield Club. But this has happened and as such I attended a lunch laid on by a well known sponsoring bank. The cold roast beef was frankly atrocious, tasteless, fatless and textureless. How can we expect to win back that one fifth of purchased meat if one of the leading banks can't get the right stuff, and at Smithfield of all places? Oh! I know you'll be saying 'It's the butchers' fault, they don't hang it enough'. True in many cases, but what about us farmers, do we breed for quality or quantity? When I say this I am not just thinking of the breed with which I had a close association for nine years. There is quality in individuals in all beef breeds, but now all too much quantity.

Also, sometimes one would think some people were paying for the daylight under the bulls they buy, judging by the daft sums paid for beasts with no backsides. Then , of course, some farmers stuff their beasts with hormones and if the animal doesn't make enough in the fat ring they take it home and give it another lot. Really, talk about the Gadarene swine, we're doing our best *not* to sell quality. Even if it's the minority that are selfish it's *too* many.

Stephen Pile of 'The Sunday Times' wrote of me, "We all looked at this grizzled old chap in a kilt who promptly padded off like a dog seeking its bone and led the Queen Mother into the carcase department'. Good for one's conceit isn't it? If ever there was an advocate for quality it is the Queen Mum. She backs beef from the breed of her choice at Castle of Mey and Clarence House. I know that at Castle of Mey the potatoes eaten are Sharpe's Express, Duke of York, Kerr's Pink and Golden Wonder, and for me what better? So it's annoying that Kerr's Pink are currently £2 per bag and imported Spanish £4. Are we using too much fertiliser and not enough dung?

The highlights of my Smithfield Show in recent years have been conducting the carol service in the main ring on the Sunday and showing the Queen Mum round the cattle lines on the Wednesday.

One remark Her Majesty passed, got me thinking what a wise old bird she is, it was, 'I can't imagine a tasty piece of beef that hasn't some fat on it and marbling through it'. Oh if only more housewives thought the same way we wouldn't be having all those fearful arguments that have been raging recently, led by what I call the 'over lean and tasteless' lobby.

Here we are in a situation where figures recently printed show that red meat consumption is falling by an alarming 5% and yet part of the beef trade are doing their best to wreck it. And don't let's fool ourselves; have we always produced the best article? Or have we not at times substituted greed for need?

Although Scots for the first time in fifteen years didn't win the overall Championship that wonderful 'extrovert veteran' Davy Sinclair took the carcase and combined live/dead award *and* charmed the Queen Mum. But for me pride of place for the award for Scot of the Year Smithfield goes to Jim Royan. I have been at the Show since 1949 and I've never seen such a polished performance in the judging ring nor such a concise summing up on the mike as to why he was placing his animals as he did. But perhaps best of all was when he said to the Press that the industry should be 'producing meat for all tastes'. That, to my mind sums it all up. But it infuriates me when our boffins tell us that we have to produce lean beef - that all too often has no taste.

How things have changed in Earls Court since I went to my first show. I showed cattle and sheep for the late Duncan Stewart, Millhills. Very few stockmen now live underground in the labyrinths that form the tunnels under Earls Court. And no longer do they have water dripping on their beds from condensation! They now have some decent cookers and washing facilities, and if they want to eat in the restaurants, the food is good but wickedly expensive. Most stockmen now stay in hotels.

I've just watched a video of 'The Farmer of the Future' running his farm from his office, by computer of course. Every shot that came up on the video showed the latest machinery, all costing tens of thousands of pounds, and this machinery was on display at the Show. When one realises that only six per cent of our land in Scotland is prime arable land on which these great monsters can work, is the show not catering for the Barley Barons? Gone are a lot of the wee stands that catered for the wee man who used buckets and graips, wheelbarrows and all the paraphernalia that comes out of the loft door on the day of a roup. Changed days!

No longer do we see our traditional breeds coming to the top, but each year sees yet another foreign name being added to the list of crosses both in sheep and cattle lines. Can it be coincidence that so many of my southern friends say they can no longer get any tasty meat? There is a lot more about Smithfield but because of the way that farming is going more and more emphasis is on the big boy whether it be Barley Baron or Super Market. I don't think all the changes have been for the good.

The Herds Fair at New Cumnock was a pleasant relief after Smithfield as it was a real dip into the old. For 200 years the herds have met to report any straggling sheep that were on their ground and if not claimed at the Fair then they were sold for charity. Because of modern transport and communications there hadn't been any straggling sheep reported since the 1930s until this year when two wether lambs were reported. I was proud to be part of the 270 people who belong to this ancient club whose minutes have been meticulously kept for all their 200 years and who still donate any surplus cash to local charity. You can't beat a gathering of herds when it comes to dancing, even although they no longer wear their 'tackity boots'.

December

That everyone likes something different was borne out to me when I had to make a speech at the Bicentenary of the Fife Foxhounds which was a super evening: 220 attended and we had a first-class meal. The main course was beef, always difficult to cook for that number. I would have preferred mine underdone but someone at my table thought it just right. It takes all sorts to make a world.

It's good to be back from Smithfield to a civilised countryside where one can live and work and have one's being; instead of being pushed and jostled around that madhouse known as London. And it's good to have a drop of decent water in one's dram instead of the stuff that's been recycled umpteen times from the Thames - and it tastes like it. A friend of mine took me in a taxi one day at lunchtime and it took us 45 minutes to go three miles. We could have walked it in the time! But everyone to his own way of life and I don't suppose the empty faces I saw would enjoy 'saucin aboot in the glaur' that makes up Woodburn these days.

I'm glad I wasn't one of the many tractor and machinery salesmen at Smithfield who were putting a brave face on what must be a poor year for them. One section of our industry which does seem to have money are the young farmers. As one of Smithfield Club's Vice Presidents I was ashamed to hear that members of the Y F C had broken up one of the bars. We are having a bad enough image painted of us by the urban population already without that sort of stuff.

Talking of our image, I wonder how many of you watched 'Cold Comfort Farm' on television a fortnight ago? I thought it was a well balanced programme that showed us in a true light. I was proud indeed that the Presenter was a summer student of mine back in 1959. The crux of the programme was: we are overproduced, but if we are to preserve our countryside as we know it, and more importantly the people who live there, what do we do with the acres that go out of use? We certainly don't want to see the ghastly mess I saw in the States back in 1959 where one passed mile after mile of waste land that had been taken out of production. A suggested answer was given by Ian Cunningham, Head of the West College of Agriculture at a seminar hosted by Perth & Kinross District Council. The seminar was on forestry planning. Ian's point was that of course it's been proved we need more timber but why should the hill farms always be the target? And if some are to be planted why not plant only parts of them

so that whole glens are not sterilised? And how about parts of arable farms which are overproducing?

It was tonic to get back from Smithfield to help run the Ardoch Agricultural Society's Whist Drive where there were 42 tables. Along with their raffle they raised £922. These are the wee shows that keep the Smithfields alive.

B S E would seem to be on everybody's lips these days. It seems to me that it has been blown out of all proportion. Who in this country eats cow brains and nerves anyway? As a shepherd on the Borders back in the 1930s, our diet was either braxy mutton or poached salmon which, by the time the salmon had reached us, was well and truly red. Scrapie was rife in those days. In fact, the late Dr. Greig of Moredun was working on the disease on the farm on which I was employed. The old housekeeper who fed us must have been one of the worst cooks it's ever been my displeasure to know (and that includes Army cooks who were in Wartime not famous for their culinary prowess!). But one thing the housekeeper *could* make was 'potted heid', and if sheep's scarpie brains could be transferred to humans then perhaps that accounts for some of my own madness. But to be serious, it's not cows that are mad but the cattle feed manufacturers who ever started to use bits of sheep in the cattle feed. It's terrible what some folk will do just to make a bit more profit. I was delighted to read in 'The Scottish Farmer' of a Speysider who is still feeding oats and neeps to his cattle. I'm a realist who hears on all sides the consumer crying out for food that is naturally produced, not necessarily organically produced.

I was sad to hear on the radio that draff will no longer be available for local farmers as it is being bought up to be made into some super protein. How I loved to go to my local distillery to collect the draff (and a glass of the clear stuff) when I was up farming in Speyside. I often wonder how much draff had to do with the excellence of the cattle from that area which has been called the 'Cradle of champions' because of the number of Smithfield Champions it has bred.

Ten days ago I had the honour to speak at the 153rd Annual Dinner of the Fettercairn Show. As in all after dinner speeches, I try to mix the serious with some humour. On the serious side, I was saying what a great part agricultural shows have to play in the life of our countryside. This is especially true of the smaller shows like Fettercairn which are set up and dismantled by committee members. At last year's show some disgruntled exhibitor said to the committee chairman (who was rightly issuing orders) 'You'd think you were God'. Back came the reply like a pistol shot 'Today laddie I *am* God'. And dead right too. One of the other serious subjects I touched on was the bad image all too many farmers give to the urban population. Some seem to revel in flaunting their worldly goods, Range Rovers, Mercedes, three nights curling etc. Why not? I hear you say, the top people in other walks of life have these things so why not us? Well there's a subtle difference in that as a breed we are well known for moaning and wingeing. You'll all know the story of the minister congratulating a farmer of his congregation on his magnificent crops in 1984, to which the farmer replied 'Aye, but it takes and awful lot oot o the Grun'.

Things are not looking good for the industry, thanks to our own efficiency. But those of us who remember the late 1920s and 1930s know they could be an awful lot worse. The worst thing as I see it is that back in those days we had lots of people in the countryside but now they have gone, never to return.

December

At this time of year we in the farming industry have so much to be thankful for. If I lived my life again I'd force my way into farming somehow not to make money but because I love the way of life and the folk in the industry. Now I'm retired I realise more than ever how many hidden benefits we enjoy. How many hidden blessings that we take for granted. Some of us still go to church to give thanks but others feel they can rub along without it.

In 1944 I was lucky enough to be given a job by the late Sir James Roberts of Strathallan. Once I'd settled down, as is my want in any new district, I joined the local Kirk which was Trinity Gask. I am once again a member of the same church after all these years of travelling around Scotland and as I sat meditating before the Christmas Eve service I thought how things have changed in the intervening years and for once, this old warhorse thinks, for the better. It may seem extraordinary to young people today but we always worked on Christmas Day. There was no Christmas Eve service and unlike this year, when I passed cottage after cottage with windows with brightly lit Christmas trees, there used to be none. Farm workers, and Farm managers' presents (if any) to their children were either boots or pieces of wearing apparel. But all these years later I stepped up the church path gaily lit with coloured lights into a warm full church where just to remind us of the past the Elders had lit the old paraffin lamps. We then had a lovely service in which we could all partake. And it was short. What a pleasant change from forty years ago!

But as I sat contemplating the age-old story of the child in the manger with the oxen looking on and the shepherds in the fields abiding I thought of the countless times farming is mentioned in the Bible. The lost sheep (as the wee schoolboy said when asked why there was so much hassle about the search 'It must be the Tup'), the sower and his seed, the vineyards, the farmer who build bigger barns and the Lord said 'Tonight I have need of thee'. And countless more. I've preached a sermon on the latter text but it was never more needed than now, when we are going to have to take a right good look at ourselves. Farming was a basic industry in Biblical times but I wish the powers that be would realise that it still is and just about the only one left, now that our coal and steel have been whittled away to a shadow of their former glory.

Good land and the farmer's boot that treads it are irreplaceable. The farming industry should heed the Old Book and not make bigger and bigger holdings. I'm all for smaller, well managed ones. That's the way to have an overdraft-free New Year!

Pussy in a sunny place: drawn by Maisie Murray.

Far From The Crowd

In January 1990 Captain Ben Coutts was featured in the BBC Scotland radio series 'Far From the Crowd'. He was interviewed by Alan Wright. The following is an edited transcript of the programme.

ALAN WRIGHT Captain Ben Coutts has lived most of his life far from the crowd in the hills and glens of Scotland and now lives in gentle retirement at Woodburn just outside Crieff. He wrote a book not so long ago which traced his life from boyhood as a son of the manse to being a groom, through hellish wartime experiences to his return to the land, through days as a Cattle Breed Society Secretary - which is likened to the job of a football team manager - to farming on his own account, from farming politics to the broader ones. The book is called *From Bothy to Big Ben*.

Ben, where did your love of the land come from?

BEN COUTTS Probably from my grandfather who was a crofter's son. They were bred up in Strathdon in Aberdeenshire. He left to be a chemist and went down to Manchester where my father was born. My father always loved the hills dearly and to his dying day did a lot of walking in them. I never thought of anything else but farming, I just adored the land and I'm a great believer in breeding. I think it comes out very strongly in us all and even people who live in Glasgow, Edinburgh or whatever town you care to name, you'll find that in their breeding somewhere they've got farming background, because after all we all came from the land originally and it does keep coming out, never stronger than in this day and age when we're seeing gardens blooming, people going into allotments, window boxes, things like that. I think you're seeing it very strongly in this country today. No doubt it came out terribly strongly in me and came out very strongly in two of my sons.

AW Can you put your finger on what's special about living in the country?

BC Oh, it's a way of life. There's something about struggling with nature. You remember 1985 when we'd that ghastly summer. I remember 1947, that terrible winter. You know these things, you come up against it and you find it's not just yourself. In business nowadays when you're working with computers and figures you can do a lot with these but when you're working with the land you're up against a challenge the whole time and I love it.

110

Far From The Crowd

Living in the country, to me, is life, It's not all beer and skittles. There's a lot of very, very hard times. But listen to the robins, that we both heard before this broadcast, the cushie doos making that lovely haunting sound they have. I just like everything about the land.

AW Is it easier to enjoy the countryside if you don't have to make a living from it at the same time?

BC I don't think so. I'm a great believer in challenge. Because of that I think I've had more out of my way of life in the country because I've had to work at it. People just coming to the country to enjoy themselves don't have that. I think I've been a terribly lucky laddie to be allowed to live a life I enjoy and at the same time make a living. Sometimes a bit precarious, I might tell you.

AW Why do you think that nowadays so many more people, the townies, are taking a keener interest in what happens in the country, almost claiming that at least part of the countryside is theirs?

BC The reason is, there's just too many people in this country. Sally and I were out in Australia last year where there's practically no people in thousands and thousands of square miles. I was coming back in the car the other night from Crieff and popping along the country road as I always do and heard on my wireless that there was a queue of five miles on the M4 and a queue of six miles on the M6. I thanked God literally that I was sitting and living where I was. The reason townies think it's as much theirs as those of us who work there is that they have this feeling of democracy - what's mine is yours and we have as much right as the other person. Which is a pity in a way because it's so essential that we in the farming industry, in the nicest possible way, instruct people from the urban population on how they should behave. We love seeing them if they behave. When I had the farm I'd a mile on a B-road. Along that mile every Autumn my old man and I used to collect a bogey load of rubbish - tins and bottles, plastic, paper, fish and chip things. How sad! Why can't they take their rubbish home? All that sort of thing, people wandering in through sheep with their dog. 'Little Fifi never looks at a sheep, she wouldn't dream of it.' What they don't realise is that sheep, because of the way they're bred, think of dogs as relations of wolves. If they see a dog they push off in a corner and if they're very heavily in lamb it can do these sheep an awful lot of harm. Stop things like that, but if they behave we love seeing them.

111

Far From The Crowd

AW In Scotland we have enjoyed more or less freedom of access so long as we're not destroying a graining crop. We can pretty much walk where we like. We don't have the antagonisms they have in England about bridal paths and footpaths and things like that.

BC The main reason, as you know, is that we don't have as many people up here as they do in the South. We don't have the antagonisms. It's only a small percentage that make it bad for the rest. I managed the Blackmount Estate up in the Bridge of Orchy for the Fleming family, the bankers, for 25 years. It's a great stalking estate, a beautiful part of the country. Old Major Fleming, before he died, said he'd had only one stalk spoilt and it wasn't even then completely spoilt. He'd been there from 1923 until he died, a good 50 years. Nowadays the West Highland Way has gone through - a marvellous idea. People get out of Glasgow, Liverpool and all these big cities and come and walk up that lovely country from Loch Lomond right up to Fort William - and it goes bang through Blackmount Estate. 99 per cent of the people behave superbly: one per cent have to push off the West Highland Way and go into the hills to see what it's all about. We've a big notice up saying, Please, if you're walking between the dates of the stalking, about 10th August - 20th October, please tell the stalker. It tells you where his house is and all the rest. But that one per cent don't bother, it's sad, they spoil it for the rest. Major Fleming was a lovely man, he always used to say, 'I love seeing people enjoy themselves'. He never turned anybody off that Estate in all the years that I looked after it for him. And his son is doing the same thing. There are hundreds of nice landlords. Again it's just a small percentage of landlords who spoil it for the rest. We do like seeing people in the country, but please will they behave themselves. There's a lovely story about a crowd of people who came and had tea in a farmer's field: he was just going to cut the hay and you know what a mess that can make in grass a foot high, suddenly flattened by those people. So he found out their car number, he checked with the police where the car came from, and it came from one of the suburbs. Off set the farmer with his family, and his picnic stuff and went to this garden and sat down to eat. The chap came out, absolutely furious. The farmer said 'Well you did exactly the same thing in my hay crop'. This is the way we have to look at it.

AW But is it right to put them all on the same path? A lot of people now think that the West Highland Way has been turned into a sort of scar across the countryside.

Far From The Crowd

BC I'm afraid that's happened. I haven't got the brain to work this one out. I understand that in the Peak District they're having terrible difficulty and there's no doubt in the West Highland Way bits that go over the peat bogs are very bad. We're lucky in the Blackmount stretch because that's the old General Wade road. How beautifully they were made, all these cassie stones put together by hand. There we've been extremely lucky, that hasn't been churned up. But where they go over peat bogs and things of that sort it's become just a morass. I honestly don't know what's going to happen. In the old days just a very few people doing what we all have to do naturally was alright, but when you have hundreds of people it's not so funny: toilets will have to be built. One group of people who have done terribly well in these places are the hotels en route, which is great. They make employment.

But what are we going to do about these hill areas? Even just after the War, when I came back, there were men up at the head of the glens, shepherds who wanted to be close to their flocks, super chaps. Television has done harm in some ways because people see another way of life that they think could be theirs. The wives very rightly say, 'Oh why can't I have a washing machine' or 'You've got to get a car Jock and the telephone' Can you blame them? We've always wanted a high standard of living and we're all trying to educate our family better that we were educated. Some move out of the rural areas to make more money. Then a lot of people are coming out of towns and settling in Highland villages, and a lot of locals call them 'White Settlers'. A lot of good has come out of this, They're finding new crafts - pottery, glass, horn sticks that shepherds have made for generations, things of that sort. Some are selling high class souvenirs. Most of that has happened from incomers. The standard of food in the Highlands, in the cafes and restaurants has improved out of all recognition, but there's a long way to go as you know. At the top of the glens the people are leaving and with them a type of person that did this country so much good, people who were bred in the glens with that hardy upbringing and a sensible outlook to nature and life and usually kirk-goers. They've done an awful lot of good in Great Britain.

AW But this drift from the land, of people who earn their living in it, isn't new.

Far From The Crowd

BC Yes, take the estate I managed for three years, it had thirty people working on it. Today there's one. In the job I had before that, managing for Sir James Robertson at Strathallan, one of the best stockers I ever had, horseman and tractorman he was, his wife was desperate to get to town. They were lured away by the motor manufacturers just after the War. I met him many years later, his wife had got all the things she wanted, but he wasn't happy. Once, too, I was up in the Black Isle, and I was taken round one or two farms, with no industry round about them at all, long before oil came into force. They had a high class labour. They went on for many years with no industry up against them, whereas round Stirling and Glasgow, with big factories going up, a lot of labour was taken away from the land.

AW The march of machinery onto farms was bound to mean that people were to go.

BC Oh absolutely, what a difference its made! You take the average shepherd I knew in the old days, he walked every inch of his hill. Nowadays they have land rovers and goodness knows what, to take them to the top. And there are all those horrible roads, I just hate seeing these roads that scar across the Highlands of Scotland. The shepherd or the stalker used to walk every inch.

We've all been softened up, I'm afraid. But machinery has done a lot of good, though some of it has been overdone. You're getting 4-wheel drive tractors now on farms where they don't need that power. It's doing the drains a lot of harm, the machinery is getting heavier and heavier. The two things that really revolutionised farming, and a boon to the farmer's wife, were, number one, electricity. Fantastic when that came in, what a difference. Instead of going out to a byre to see a cow calving with the old paraffin lamp, which is beautifully romantic, I love the smell of it, and the smell of the byre and the stable. But to click on that light and click it off again and go back to your bed is marvellous. Electric blankets, when you were out to a calving and came back to that - oh great. Now these things, for the wife and in the kitchen, what a difference! And the other thing, number two, was the three-point linkage first seen on the Harry Ferguson tractor: that revolutionised things too. It made an awful difference to our life.

114

Far From The Crowd

You know these great big round bales you see in fields nowadays, well they're not very useful for feeding a horse or two. Horses need hay. You can't buy these huge whacking bales. And so many people have gone out of square bales. You can hardly find any now. An old chap I worked for always said 'When they're aa going west laddie, you go east'. And it's so right. Now some farmers are producing small bales for ever-increasing horse numbers.

AW The greatest change probably in your lifetime must have been this moving after the War from a position where we nearly starved to a position now with our colleagues in the Common Market where we've produced too much food.

BC I wonder if there's all the food about that people are shouting about. We hear about these grain mountains. I understand, on very good authority, that there's only enough grain left to last us ten days or something if anything ghastly hits the world. In Scotland we have had, as you know, some very bad harvests. Last year was marvellous in a way but then some people had bad harvests because they had a drought. We are talking about this set-aside, which I think is a disaster. There's great talk about this greenhouse effect. I've stood in queues, for my parents in wartime, and I never want to see this happen in this country again. I would much rather see a country of people with filled bellies than people standing in queues, and you only have to look into Europe now and see them doing this in Hungary and Poland and places. I think that all these things together could quite easily bring about food queues. We're only guessing at a lot of it, but it wouldn't take a lot, just a few percentages off our arable acreage as it stands today, for us to be in real trouble.

AW You've done broadcasts about farming in the countryside for 40 years now. They started at Oban. How did they start?

BC I was managing Millhills Estate which at that time had the famous Short Horn Cattle. They were, the red roans and the white, the basis of our beef cattle in this country if you like. At that time, just after the War, they were very much in demand in Argentina, the States and Canada and we at Millhills were one of the top herds. I was sent by my then boss, Duncan Stewart, to go to a sale in Calrossie in Ross-shire where there was a very famous herd. My boss was very interested in a bull there. He told me the

115

amount of money that we could go to in order to buy it, but actually the bull was retained by its owner. He only had it there for show. But anyway when I was there I met the then agricultural producer Alasdair Dunnett. Alasdair couldn't go on to Oban. We had not only a herd of Shorthorn cattle but what we call a fold of Highland cattle on the hills at Carse, and we had some heifers to be sold in Oban so I had to go from Kilrossie across to Oban. Alasdair said he was desperately keen to get the Oban results, would I be good enough to put them down to the BBC for him. I said 'What do I do?' and he said 'Oh you reverse the charge down to Edinburgh and get on the phone'. I had the most terrible butterflies, I remember, I get them to this day just doing this. I got to Oban and I remember somebody saying to me, 'Ben, if you can possibly put in a wee story or a crack people will enjoy it'. Old Jimmy Bain, the cattle dealer, and I were talking that day and it was coming down whole waters, as it can in Oban. There's an island off Oban, in the bay called Kerra, and Jimmy said to me 'Ay ay Ben it's the usual sort of Oban weather, if ye can't see Kerra it's raining and if you can, it's going to!' That was the start of the broadcast 40 years ago and I thank Jimmy for it, because it relieved the tension.

AW   What sort of things are you broadcasting about nowadays then?

BC   I like to bring out from my experiences, where I've gone wrong, and perhaps the farming industry has gone wrong, or sometimes how we from the past certainly can learn a lot from the modern generation of farmers. But I think the modern generation can learn a lot from the older generation. Everyone's in such a hurry nowadays, especially so far as stock are concerned. You don't become a stocks man overnight. It takes a long time. You've really got to study them and you can't rush at it.

AW   In this long and terribly varied life, you've been everything from military career to Breed Society Secretary, from farming on your own account to farming big estates for other people. What was the happiest time in all that?

BC   If I was given my life over again, I don't think I'd change any of it, even getting my nose blown off, because in a funny old way it gave me self confidence that I never had before. I was a terribly shy chap before that. Probably the happiest time was when I was in the bothy as a groom. You'd no responsibilities. I was a Sergeant-Major, then a Captain, then managing a lot of men, so the buck stopped at me. When I was a Sergeant-Major the Colonel said to me, 'I'm afraid you've got to take a commission', and I said 'Oh no sir I'm happy here'. He said 'You're shirking your responsibilities'. Dead right. That's why I was happy as a groom. I hadn't any, and I was pretty good at the job, I think, because I really should have been doing a bigger job. That's not the way you should be living your life. We're all given gifts and we should use them.

AW What was the happiest day in your life?

BC There's more than one. I think two of the happiest days were organising two cattle sales. I had a herd of cattle at Gaskbeg and a herd of cattle here. I love organising things. I organised these two sales and thanks to the money I made from them I was able to educate my family and I was very proud here when the chief yardsman from McDonald-Fraser who conducted the sale said it was the best conducted sale he'd ever known. I'm a conceited chap at the best of times and that really put me over the moon. These were two great days. And I must say this, again conceited - I just love Queen Elizabeth the Queen Mother. The ten years I was Secretary of the Aberdeen-Angus Society she always asked myself and my president to go through the cattle and have lunch with her. When I gave up I got an invitation to go. I said, sorry I was no longer Secretary and the new Secretary should be asked, which he was. Well, within a week there was an invitation from the Queen Mother to go and bring Sally with me, which had never happened in the past. When I had gone up to the Castle to see the cattle it was absolutely on business. Sally and I went to Birkhall. The Queen Mother has a lovely fishing lodge there, given to her on her eightieth birthday by her family. There she was herself having what she called a picnic. There as well was Princess Alice and Princess Alexandra and Angus Ogilvy. It was a lovely, lovely happy day and I'll die a happy man thinking of that.